THE GREEN MAN MYTH AND REALITY

IMOGEN CORRIGAN

First published 2025

Amberley Publishing
The Hill, Stroud,
Gloucestershire, GL5 4EP

www.amberley-books.com

ISBN: 978 1 3981 1690 0 (print)
ISBN: 978 1 3981 1691 7 (ebook)

British Library Cataloguing in Publication Data.
A catalogue record for this book is available from the British Library.

Typeset in 10pt on 13pt Celeste.
Origination by Amberley Publishing.
Printed in the UK.

EU GPSR Authorised Representative
Appointed EU Representative: Easy Access System Europe Oü, 16879218
Address: Mustamäe tee 50, 10621, Tallinn, Estonia
Contact Details: gpsr.requests@easproject.com, +358 40 500 3575

Contents

Introduction

In the 1930s two well-known and respected folklorists stood in St Jerome's Church in Llangwym, Monmouthshire, discussing a particular foliate head carving. One was the vicar, Revd J. Griffith, who suggested that it was intended to symbolise the spirit of inspiration, but to the other, Lady Raglan, 'it seemed certain that it was a man and not a spirit. And moreover, that it was a Green Man. So I named it.' She wrote about this encounter later in 1939 and so the name passed into general currency. Quite how and why it became popular so quickly is not clear, but it did, and this almost catapulted the image into the forefront of people's imagination.

So, what is this figure that was to become so controversial? It is in every medium. It is found carved in wood or stone or perhaps painted on glass or in a manuscript. It has occasionally been found on medieval encaustic floor tiles. The image under discussion in this book can be found anywhere in or on a church or cathedral. They are usually disembodied heads, but not always, and they can be highly stylised. They have foliage or occasionally something unexpected issuing from the mouth, nose, ears, eyes, or a combination of those orifices. These types are known as disgorging heads, as at Salhouse and Claypole. There are also the so-called transformers, which are more artistic to look at and involve the head either transforming into foliage or perhaps they have foliage growing from their forehead or face. There are variations on these themes; very often a head might be both disgorging and transforming, most usually with foliage growing out of its forehead. Elsewhere we might find examples of heads whose hair and/or moustaches and beards might transform into foliage, such as at Maidstone and Pershore, a design very similar to one at Stratford-upon-Avon (an image that must surely have been seen by Shakespeare).

In this book the focus will mainly be on those discovered in churches and a few cathedrals in England, although they are found right across what was the Catholic West (more or less the area of modern Europe), and there are secular examples too. It only appears to be in Britain that there is widespread interest in the Green Man and that has to be because of Lady Raglan. Her naming of it was to be one of the most important things in its history, simply because it triggered a wave of interest that is not found on the Continent. There appears to have been an equal dearth of interest in this country before she did so. Neither the name nor the level of interest have travelled overseas. Were you to go into a

Pembrokeshire, Llangwm, St Jerome, *c.* 1500.

Tewkesbury Abbey.
Copy of a medieval
encaustic floor tile.

Norfolk, Salhouse, All Saints, *c.* 1400.
Disgorging head.

Lincolnshire, Claypole, St Peter, *c.* 1300.
Disgorging head.

Norfolk, Necton, All Saints, 1410.
Transforming head.

Norfolk, Scottow, All
Saints, *c.* 1400.
Transforming head.

Suffolk, Bardwell, St Peter and St Paul, *c.* 1400.
Disgorging and transforming head.

Lincolnshire,
Brant Broughton,
St Helen, *c.* 1400.
Disgorging and
transforming head.

Kent, Maidstone,
All Saints, early
fifteenth century.
Hair transformer.

Worcestershire,
Pershore Abbey,
Holy Cross,
c. 1350.
Hair transformer.

French church, for example, and ask to see the *Homme Vert*, you would be met with blank looks – this has been tried several times. Even asking about the *tête-de-feuille* (the leafy head) does not reap much enthusiasm or even knowledge as to what you are talking about. It is just a carving, and yet it is one that is found in several forms in and on 4 to 5 per cent of our parish churches and at least one (if not many) can be spotted in or on every cathedral that had the status of cathedral before the Reformation of the 1530s, not just in Britain, but right across Europe. This breakdown is in itself remarkable. The prevalence of them in cathedrals indicates something either of status or of enhanced importance about them. Although it is routinely found in cathedrals, it is the only thing we have trouble in explaining. We can describe the use of an altar or pulpit and the imagery in windows and wall paintings, but the precise function of the Green Man eludes us.

The notion of the Green Man (more accurately, but less enticingly, called a foliate head) continues to attract people right up to the present day. A lot has been written about it, especially in the last two decades, but its name has caused some people to try to attach spiritual or folkloric ideas to it that were never intended by the medieval makers. Others have seen it as part of a comparatively modern spiritual awakening. One of the aims of this book is to try to set the record straight, so to speak. To try to find out why it evidently was an accepted and important image, how the misinterpretations set in, where it came from and to try to analyse what it stood for. It certainly must have stood for something. These are not doodles made by chance or on a whim and they were created in days when religious symbolism was relevant and mattered.

It is also such a common motif that it must have a function that is more than merely decorative, although it is accepted that there was a medieval delight in depicting monsters of many types, so you could argue that this is just one of them. That said, it should not be dismissed as merely being a strange liminal image, carved almost as some sort of filler or afterthought. Many examples are found at thresholds and in the less-accessible parts of the buildings, but others are also found right at the heart of the sacred space. This is something that will be looked at in more detail, but it is important to say at the outset that these heads were made at a time when Catholic Christian religious practice was an important part of daily life and belief in an afterlife mattered. A prevailing thought was that the only reason anyone existed in this life was to try to get into the next one; it was their duty and their joy to do so.

That does not mean that the foliate head as an idea was exclusive to Christianity. It certainly dates back to pagan times, but then so do many things in our churches such as labyrinths, dragons and numerous monsters. Pagan images were regularly harnessed to help to tell the Christian story. Indeed, Pope Gregory the Great (AD 540–604) routinely advised evangelists such as Mellitus to be wary of offending those whom he had been sent to convert. In effect, they should not trash pagan practices, images and activities but look to see how they could be used to tell the Christian story and bring the pagan into what Gregory saw as being the true faith. In this way numerous once-pagan images and some from classical times found their way into the visual language of the church. Foliate heads are part of this tradition but at the time the images of this study were created, they were being used in an exclusively Christian context. As often happens, the images might not descend from one single point in a direct line, but perhaps are a merger of ideas from classical, Asian, Celtic and indeed folkloric starting points.

One of the things that quickly becomes apparent is that Green Men are neither green nor necessarily men. An extensive study was made for this book; indeed, about a thousand parish churches and cathedrals across the nation and in every county were scrutinised and a huge variety of representations were found (there is not a county that does not have any). Approximately 55 per cent are identifiable as human. It is not always possible to assign gender to these heads, although, presumably because of the name Lady Raglan bestowed on them, several writers claim that they are male. It is usually impossible to be sure. The remaining heads are either recognisable animals, fictional beasts or grotesques with some being too eroded to be able to tell. Some of these creatures were symbolic. It is rare for original colour to remain (some have been restored) but it is not thought that the colour green is relevant in itself; where there is original colour it is predominantly red or gold. Some have traces of green but it is never the main colour and where green does predominate, it is normally the result of a post-1939 refurbishment. That said, foliage is key to their design and interpretation even if the various types of it might not be.

As churches were inspected, other things became apparent too. The foliate head carvings were often part of a suite of images, which occurred especially on columns near or at the chancel arch and on fonts. This was a great help because it was often possible to analyse those other images to decide if they were symbolic and in what sense. This is something that this book will examine because it offers the most substantial clues as to what the carvings represented. It became obvious that the Green Man being part of a story, as it were, is something that occurred more often in the earlier part of the Middle Ages than

Yorkshire, Beverley, St Mary, *c.* 1400.
A human foliate head.

Lincolnshire, Greatford, St Thomas Becket, fourteenth century.
Although eroded now, it is possible to make out the head shape and leaves.

Kent, Wingham, St Mary, *c.* 1340.
A horse-like disgorging animal.

Yorkshire, York, All Saints, North Street, fifteenth century. An image that has been restored relatively recently. The foliage is green, but the face is golden.

later. Towards the end (the early to mid-sixteenth century) it was more likely that the head would have been carved as a separate entity. This does not imply that they were standing alone, but that they were not so bound up with other imagery. This might in turn suggest that by that time it was widely known what they were for. The same phenomenon occurs in medieval manuscripts where it is more likely to find foliate heads, sometimes in highly stylised forms in the margins of earlier rather than later works. Green Men in manuscripts potentially make an interesting study since they are inextricably caught up in the Word of God. If they are in or on churches then plainly they are hosted by the house of God, but there is a difference between that and the sacred Word especially in the Middle Ages when the Word could only by interpreted by priests who had been trained in theology. No one could interfere with the Word without peril and to have it translated into the vernacular was considered to be a heresy. And yet we see foliate heads not just playing alongside other monsters, but occasionally as part of a text praising a senior churchman as in the *Codex Egberti* (Trier Cod.24) made in the monastery at Reichenau for Egbert, bishop of Trier at the end of the tenth century. That elevates the image to something almost laudatory and perhaps puts them in the same bracket as ones found on tombs.

Monasteries were not strangers to foliate heads. They do not form a part of this book simply because, in Britain at least, so many of them have fallen into ruin that it is impossible to make a reasonable judgement as to how they were normally used for decoration and how they were placed. Enough examples have been found either on column capitals or even on the late twelfth-century stone lectern of Wenlock Priory (now in the Victoria and Albert Museum) to see that they were not an uncommon feature. That said, monastery churches, which often doubled as parish churches, did host foliate heads, as can be seen at Boxgrove, Croyland, Fountains Abbey, Lacock, Leominster, Pershore, Romsey, Sherborne and Tewkesbury to name only a few.

Locations became a big part of the research. Inevitably geography came into it because of the logistics of visiting likely churches in each part of the realm. Churches became prospective candidates for examination if they featured in gazetteers about Green Men or were on relevant websites. A possible Green Man might be spotted in a book about misericords, fonts or other carvings, or someone might have mentioned that there was one in situ and so that church went on the list to be visited, often with mixed results. There is certainly plenty of scope. According to the English Church Census of 2005, there are 16,247 Anglican churches in England. It has not been possible to obtain an accurate figure of how many of these were founded before the Reformation of the 1530s, but examination of the diocesan registers for Canterbury, Derby, Hereford, Lichfield, Norwich, Rochester and Truro indicates that it is roughly two-thirds of them, or about 10,700. As 1,384 churches were inspected, that means that only just under 13 per cent of medieval churches in England have been visited.

Naturally when hunting Green Men, a note was made as to precisely where they were in or on the church which became surprisingly interesting, especially since trends changed as time passed. With practice it obviously became easier to find the images, but it became clear that if one knew the approximate date it had been made it was all the easier to locate. The where's and why's of foliate head carvings will be looked at in some detail in a later chapter.

Lincolnshire, Croyland
Abbey, St Mary,
St Bartholomew and
St Guthlac, mid-fifteenth
century.
A monastic church.

Dorset, Sherborne Abbey, St Mary, *c.* 1200.
A monastic foundation.

Yorkshire, Fountains
Abbey, St Mary, late
fifteenth century.
Once an
important abbey.

Some writers show emotion and strong spiritual feeling in their work, a lot of which has been highly subjective. Perhaps that should be forgiven because – so far – not one primary source has been found about them. Not one record from the time when they were created has survived, whether in the form of a contract or invoice. They do not appear in bestiaries (books that allocate characteristics to animals and monsters and describe their function) or in sermons. References in medieval literature do not apply to the subject in hand. There are a few thirteenth-century drawings by Villard de Honnecourt which at least show that foliate heads were taken seriously by craftsmen. That is all. But we do have thousands of actual Green Men created in our church buildings; these numerous carvings and images must act as our primary source. This is not always straightforward because it is not unusual for the original site to have been substantially altered over the centuries. At the outset of the research, it was speculated that something could be learned by examining what the head was looking at, but this proved to be fruitless. Obviously, it could not be successfully applied to misericord carvings which are often facedown to the floor, but there are plenty of cases where the foliate head has been moved or more likely that a chapel, substantial tomb or doorway has been added to the building. A new roof must sometimes have been the death knell of heads semi-hidden in the rafters.

Kent, Minster-in-Thanet, St Mary, *c.* 1410.
Misericords in up and down positions.

Kent, Minster-in-Thanet, St Mary, *c.* 1410.
Misericord.

What has been lacking thus far is a forensic study and attempt to analyse what we see today in the context of when they were made. Foliate heads are part of the mischievous miscellany of monsters that romp through our ecclesiastic buildings and manuscripts. They need to be looked at as part of that gathering, but there is little doubt that they have a significance all of their own whether it was spiritual, talismanic or apotropaic and that they were part of the psyche of our medieval ancestors.

A specific origin of the foliate head has not yet been pinned down: it might be in folklore, classical mythology as well as in other cultures. This is, nonetheless, going to be an important part of the examination, not only because it can reveal different artistic styles combining in a single image, but because it shows a diverse background which can lead to varying interpretations. There has been some investigation into this in the past but, in general, there has been a lack of critical debate about the image and it quickly became clear that very little academic interest has been taken in the foliate head which is intriguing in itself. Writers on antiquities and church architecture routinely ignored foliate heads even though illustrations occasionally showed that the heads were evident. Thomas Rickman (1776–1841) described types of architecture and made some exquisite drawings of Dorchester Abbey which plainly shows the head we see today but he does not mention it. The same applies to G. R. Lewis who described the Shobdon folly arches in Herefordshire in 1852. It is only through his drawings that we can see the now much-eroded foliate heads in all their glory. Even more intriguingly, Pugin designed the neo-Gothic church at Ramsgate

18

Oxfordshire, Dorchester Abbey, St Peter and St Paul, thirteenth century.

and included two foliate heads, one each side of the chancel arch, but in his writing he does not refer to them at all. Foliate heads were routinely ignored, especially in the Victorian and Edwardian period when they tended to eschew images that seemed chaotic and inexplicable. It is true that Green Men are found in and on neo-Gothic buildings, but always somehow tidied-up with comparatively benign expressions that are at odds with their medieval ancestors. Victorian and earlier writers also paid scant attention to monsters and abstract images which had no overtly religious significance. This went on until well into the twentieth century when interest may well have been triggered by Lady Raglan calling them Green Men. But for her, they might have remained obscure and unremarked as they so often are in other countries.

1

Varied Beginnings and Folklore

It is intriguing that images carved in stone or wood mainly in Christian buildings perhaps 500 or even a thousand years ago have become a constant source of fascination to many and have been open to misinterpretation, misrepresentation and misunderstanding with people deciding somewhat arbitrarily that they represent pagan fertility rites. Although they have popularly become known as Green Men, technically they are 'foliate heads' and they will be referred to variously as Green Men or foliate heads, or even just as heads, throughout this book.

This idea of pagan forebears and what has been referred to as a misinterpretation needs to be explored and explained as far as it can be. It has already been mentioned that the title of Green Man was allocated by Lady Raglan in 1939. No one called it that before that date and, it seems nor did anyone outside Britain call it anything other than a foliating or leafy head. It is also apparent that no one was particularly interested in them until the name of Green Man caught the public imagination.

Nevertheless, this very name presents a problem simply because there were already noteworthy green men established in British folklore. Some of these may be modern takes on ancient customs, but they spring from the same root. For example, individuals dress as a tree, either on May Day or, these days, more often on the first Saturday in May and they lead processions down high streets accompanied by Morris dancers, musicians and mummers to bring good cheer and welcome spring. Elsewhere, a person dressed entirely in green signifying spring might fight with someone representing winter to see off a season of cold, wet and windy dreariness and ready us for more relaxed times ahead.

Although its modern name was not coined until just before the Second World War, almost every writer on the subject after that time explores the symbolism of the colour green which cannot be relevant in the context of carvings made hundreds of years before that. Some have drawn parallels with a chivalric romance written around the year 1300 which happens to be called *Sir Gawain and the Green Knight* and it is true that both Sir Gawain and his horse and their apparel were green, but no foliage is mentioned. When lecturing on this subject the author has noticed that occasionally individuals get hung up on this idea. It is almost a shame that the medieval poet used the colour green; had he used any other colour at all this distraction would not exist. Nor does it help that a smattering of characters called green men have been found in other medieval dramas. In John Kirke's play *The Seven Champions of Christendome*, written in 1638, the Clown questions a foreigner, 'Have you any squibs in your Country? Any Green-men in your shows?' These green men were especially associated with the Lord Mayor of London's Pageant where they functioned as whifflers; exotically garbed men whose role was to clear a way through the throng for the pageant-proper with the aid of branches, flaming torches and fireworks. They make another appearance in Matthew Taubman's 1686 description of the Lord Mayor's Pageant: 'In front of all these, twenty Savages or Green Men, with Squibs and Fire-works, to sweep the Streets, and keep off the Crowd.'

A couple of images have been found that qualify as being foliate heads but might in fact be whifflers; neither of them are standard. There is a carving behind the fourteenth-century stalls in Winchester Cathedral that shows a whole person with somewhat bouffant hair and who has foliage coming out of his mouth. He holds a teeny sword and shield which are plainly more likely to be theatrical props than weapons. There are other foliating images in the stalls so perhaps this particular one is a combination of foliate head and whiffler. The other image is more complex and is at Crowcombe in Somerset and dates to 1534, right on the cusp of the Reformation. Again, there is more than one foliating figure in this church, but it has been suggested that the mermen-like people coming out the ears might represent whifflers, not least because they also appear to be holding branches and somewhat floral-looking shields. Stylised vines come out of the head's mouth which can represent the Eucharistic wine or perhaps – in this case – wine drunk at a social gathering. It seems that the whifflers were expected to act as though they were very drunk and this in turn links them to breweries, which often took them as emblems as far back at the seventeenth century (after the heyday of these church carvings). It is not unusual to find pubs called The Green Man, but investigation has shown that if a pre-war picture of the sign survives, it is invariably the whiffler or perhaps the Jack-in-the-Green character associated with May Day merriment (and drinking). It was only after Lady Raglan renamed the carvings as Green Men that pub-sign images began to change.

Other legends are available, of course. One idea is that the image derived from a Roman spirit of the woods called Silvanus (which means 'of the woods', but that is a red herring). A carving of the minor Roman god Silvanus has caused a little confusion because of a fountain basin at the abbey of Saint-Denis, north-east of Paris, which shows him with oak leaves growing from his brow and an inscription bearing his name. It seems likely that this is not a link to future foliate heads, but merely a carver interpreting the Roman god of uncultivated lands, woods, agriculture, hunting and boundaries in his own way. This particular god's cult was mainly centred in Italy but gets almost no attention in literature because he was for private, not public, devotion. He is more usually shown dressed as a hunter, carrying a bow.

A separate strand of investigation comes from later Christianity in Italy but from the thirteenth-century *The Golden Legend*. It should be noted that the compiler of *The Golden Legend*, Jacobus de Voragine, did not finish his task until about the year 1266, so if the publication of the book was also the first time the narrative was heard, then it could not have had a bearing on the early foliate heads which appeared in England around the turn of the first millennium, although the stories may have been current for decades, if not

Hampshire, Winchester Cathedral, St Swithun, 1308.
Whole man with shield and sword.

Somerset, Crowcombe, Holy Ghost, 1534.
Bench-end foliate head with mermen coming out of
his ears.

London, Greene Man pub,
Euston Road.

centuries (Voragine claimed to have compiled his book from presumably now lost sources in the Vatican). His section on the Invention of the True Cross tells how when Adam was dying he sent his son, Seth, to the Garden of Eden to ask for seeds from the tree of mercy. These were laid under Adam's tongue when he was buried:

> And out of his mouth grew three trees of the three grains, of which trees the cross that our Lord suffered his passion on was made, by virtue of which he gat very mercy, and was brought out of the darkness into the very light of heaven.

It is not known when or where the story about Adam's death was first conceived, but the idea of trees growing out of Adam's mouth cannot be ignored when considering the origin of the foliate head.

Between 1890 and 1915 Sir James Frazer published *The Golden Bough*, a comprehensive examination of symbolic behaviour and folkloric practices in twelve volumes. This epic work considered numerous folk tales along with aspects of sympathetic magic and myth. In particular, Frazer explored ideas about the spirit of the tree and tree worship which would have been natural practice given that the area now known as Europe was once covered with primeval forests. Leaving aside the effect this must have had on group and individual imagination, the tree was all-important as a provider of shelter, heat, weaponry and some food as well, so it is perhaps unremarkable that it was both feared and honoured, whilst also given human characteristics and spirituality.

Frazer suggested that the spirit could be in human form in the sense of it being acted out in pageants or, perhaps, in the form of a doll incorporated in the decorations. Belief that a tree was sentient was not uncommon and Frazer's work rekindled interest in folkloric practices across Europe. His book aroused so much interest that its influence on interpretations of the foliate head should not be underestimated but it must be remembered that his interest was in folklore, rather than church sculpture. The direct link others have found between these newly identified customs and images placed in churches is entirely unproven, but Frazer's persuasive writing coloured any study of what became known as the Green Man, perhaps because it appealed to romantic notions of an idyllic past. It seems likely that Lady Raglan, herself a noted folklorist, was influenced by Frazer's ideas.

An outcome of this was that in the second part of the twentieth century the idea of Green Men appealed both to modern-day pagans and to those interested in a New Age interpretation of medieval art. This has led to foliate heads sometimes being seen as manifestations of pagan fertility rites largely based on the colour green representing fecundity and the fickleness of mankind. It is noteworthy that since foliate heads have been known as Green Men they have fired imagination, caused ideas of ownership and sparked both debate and unsubstantiated sentiments. There are numerous examples of otherwise realistic writers seeing human characteristics and emotions in the carvings and these have blurred whatever the true meaning and function may have been. It is not uncommon to see notices in churches which house foliate heads stating, for example, that the image is a fertility spirit or connected to nature and that it survives as a symbol of pre-Christian traditions. One notice further states that early builders had doubts about the long-term viability of Christianity and so added pagan symbols to placate the old gods. This is an extraordinary comment, not least because that particular church was founded in the seventh century but largely rebuilt in the twelfth century. The style of the foliate head in this church is similar to that found in the fourteenth century when builders should have felt more confidence in the no longer new religion lasting.

The oldest foliate head that has been found in a Christian context is on the tomb of St Abre in Saint-Hilaire's church in Poitiers, made *c.* AD 360. It is at her feet and is a discernibly human head which has stylised acanthus coming from the nostrils. The plant not only symbolises eternal life (apparently it is hard to get rid of it if you have it in your garden!) but this one shows notches that indicate spurts of new life. There are many examples of both pre-Christian and non-Christian heads such as one found in a museum in Amasya, northern Turkey, which dates to between 1190 and 490 BC. It is a water sprinkler used in procession, but the image is ambiguous since it could merely show a horse chewing on leaves. This is a problem when trying to trace the origin of the Green Man since there have naturally been many variations on the theme over the centuries. A better example might be the mosaic head at Herculaneum, which has to have been made before AD 79, which shows a man with a distinctly leafy moustache. Other instances include the Great Tray in the British Museum, a large plate nearly 2 feet across that features Bacchanalian scenes. In the centre is a head probably of Oceanus, a marine deity whose beard is made of seaweed and who has birds' heads coming from the edges of his mouth. The point about this fourth-century Roman dish is that it was found in England and therefore could have been an inspiration for other art forms. Heads and leaf masks with stylised but luxurious foliage are also found in Roman mosaics and they in turn may have been influenced by Greek myths and legends.

France, Poitiers, Saint-Hilaire, *c.* 360.
Tomb of St Abre.

Turkey, Amasya,
1190–490 BC.
Processional
water sprinkler.
(Rython)

Italy, Herculaneum, first century. (Photograph: Steve Delia)

Some Greek and Roman theatrical masks can also look a little like later foliate heads. The masks are necessarily disembodied heads and these have wide, aggressively shaped mouths, staring eyes, lined faces and they both have hair that could easily be interpreted as being vegetal. It was not unusual for Roman mosaicists to include masks in their work and some have leafy headdresses and/or beards made of acanthus leaves. Another example of this can be found in the Great Palace Mosaics in Constantinople which were laid down in the reign of Justinian I (AD 527–565) and at Sinop on the northern Turkish coast. Travellers from Byzantium or the northern Mediterranean area might well have brought artistic ideas with them which could be used in a different context. We know that people did travel long distances; the vast array of treasures found at Sutton Hoo in East Anglia in the ship burial of *c.* 615 reveals items from Syria, Egypt, Sweden, Germany and France and it has been established that every one of the thousands of garnets buried at the beginning of the seventh century came from India. Much later Crusaders formed an almost continual flow of traffic to and from the Middle East, staging through Constantinople where they will have seen the many glorious and exotic images adorning temples and even the sixth-century water cistern.

Or perhaps the starting points for what are now Green Men were in Scandinavia, the Celtic peoples or even India. If the origins are to be found in Indian art and sculpture then it would be more likely to have been from images that were seen rather than from legends. One possibility is the *tirthankeras,* who were the supreme preachers of Dharma who had

Turkey, Sinop, fourth century.
Mosaic.

conquered the cycle of death and rebirth and made a path for others to follow. Another possibility is the *kirttimukha,* or Face of Glory, which is often found over the doors of banks, shops and libraries today all over India and Nepal. The *kirttimukha* might be saluted before beginning a journey or before starting any great task; that is not how the foliate head was used in the Catholic West, but the carvings are remarkably similar. The Indian ones have bulging eyes, teeth in the upper jaw and stylised foliage coming from the sides of their mouths. The stylisation takes the form of granulation (a single row of beads between two lines) which is a pattern frequently seen in both Greek and Scandinavian art. That could almost be a description of heads found on a twelfth-century font at Holt in Worcestershire, a corbel in Sandwich in Kent and a capital in Southwell, also twelfth century.

As with Indian *kirttimukhas,* Celtic images had a certain consistency about them. Human images, in the sense of the whole body being shown, are rare in Celtic traditions, but the head is a recurrent symbol and the faces of the heads are often mask-like. Some of these images date as far back as the fifth century BC. In this country the term Celtic implies the culture and art of people living on the borders of Britain but in this context it means those living in central Europe. There the cult of the head was important as was an artistic style known as La Tène, named after an archaeological site in Switzerland. The La Tène style may have had an impact on the development of the foliate head largely because of its ambiguity, often hinting at an animal or human form which was suggested by swirls and spirals. For example, a first-century BC mirror back found at Aston in Herefordshire has a design which only really consists of two eye-shaped ovals at the top which are linked

India, Deccan, AD 1000–1100.
Jain tirthankeras. (Copyright Trustees of the British Museum)

Nottinghamshire,
Southwell Minster,
St Mary, twelfth
century.
Corbel beside a door.
(With kind permission
of Southwell
Cathedral Chapter)

Worcestershire, Holt, St Martin, twelfth century.
Font.

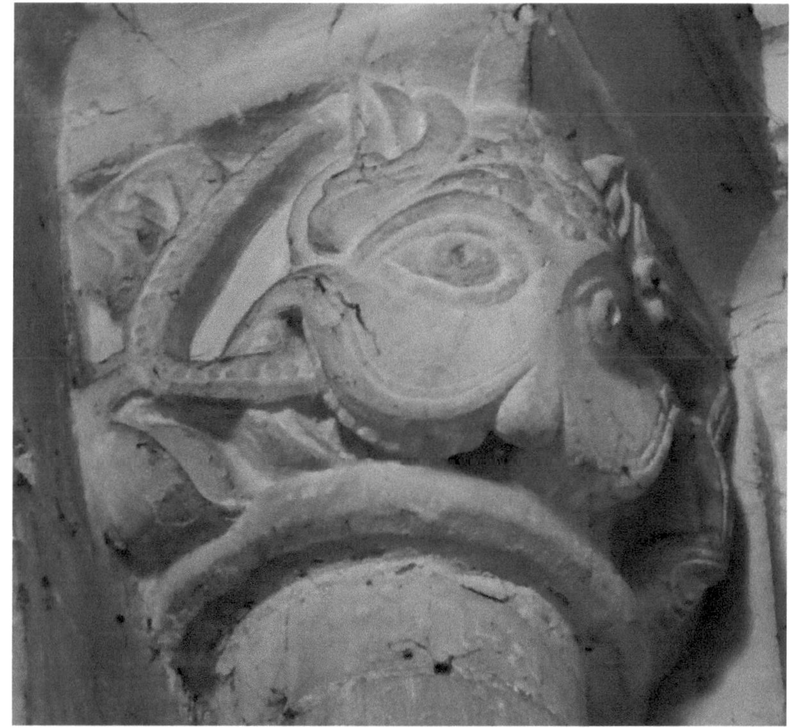

Kent, Sandwich,
St Clement, twelfth
century.
Corbels at
chancel arch.

downwards via what could be a bulbous nose to an open, circular mouth. It could be a face as is strongly suggested, but it could also just be a pattern. Triskeles, also so often seen in Scandinavian art, spirals, scrolls and swastikas were a part of this art form, as were delicate tendrils and a generally flowing and rhythmic overall design. These wispy tendrils could have been adopted by the carvers of foliate heads and some of them could be issuing from the mouths or nose. The designs are so intricate that it can be very difficult to discern precisely what is going on. Granulation, already noted, is in the Celtic portfolio of patterns; another possible influence on the earlier foliate heads. It is also noticeable that La Tène art inclined towards faces with pointed ears and hair and beards taking on a vegetal form. Faces with pointed, beast-like ears are very common amongst the foliate heads made before about the year 1200 with instances being found at twenty churches ranging from Brough in Cumbria, Alne and Felixkirk in Yorkshire to Barfrestone and Patrixbourne in Kent. Examples have also been found in Buckinghamshire, Cambridgeshire, Gloucestershire, Herefordshire, Oxfordshire, Rutland, Shropshire, Somerset, Sussex and Worcestershire.

Another branch of Celtic art, the Waldalgeshein style, named after a Rhineland grave, used palmettes and foliage worked into repetitive continuous chains which sometimes had vegetal motifs, some of which seem to transform into human faces. A repeating image in a chain of possible faces and foliage is another theme that occurs in early foliate heads, especially those on fonts.

The popular idea of links between trees and foliate heads has been explored already, but the idea of a hallowed tree should not be dismissed entirely when thinking about Celtic influences. The idea of the Tree of Life may have derived from the sheltering and

Yorkshire, Alne, St Mary, twelfth century.
Font.

Kent, Barfrestone, St Nicholas, twelfth century.
Exterior corbel.

Powys,
Brecon
Cathedral,
St John the
Evangelist,
twelfth
century.
Font.

Shrops,
Morville,
St Gregory,
post-1118.
Font.

providing nature of trees, whether in terms of fruit or timber; this is an image much used in Christianity, often on a tympanum over a door as at Kilpeck.

If the Celtic triskele transferred easily into Scandinavian art where it became widely popular, then so did spirals and scrolls. The triskele does not look dissimilar to the three-legged image on the flags of the Isle of Man and Sicily. It has a symmetry in its rotation and, instead of legs, it has spirals or coils which extend from the triangular centre of the image. It is an image that is frequently found in, for example, the Lindisfarne Gospels that date to *c.* AD 700. It is not known if this is therefore a Celtic influence or an idea that came to Britain via traders from Scandinavia before the Viking Age, the start of which is usually dated to the attack on Lindisfarne in June AD 793. The idea of the tree was important to the Vikings anyway, the cosmic world being centred on Yggdrasil, the sacred ash tree.

It is evident from manuscripts of the time such as the Durham Gospels, the Book of Durrow, the Lindisfarne Gospels, the Gospels of St Chad and the Book of Kells amongst others and from items of jewellery such as the Brooch of Tara that many of the themes already mentioned were beginning to emerge in British art. The Scandinavians – or Danes as they are called in the chronicles of the time, even if they were not from Denmark – had a great impact on British church art right up until about the year 1200 when fashions began to change. The beginning of this may be traced to the ship burial at Sutton Hoo in Suffolk of *c.* 615 which has many Swedish traits. As there is no reference to a major battle

Herefordshire, Kilpeck, St Mary and St David, twelfth century.
Tree of Life on tympanum.

in the Anglo-Saxon Chronicles or elsewhere, there must have been a peaceful migration of a Swedish dynasty which then integrated successfully into the tribes of East Anglia, ultimately coming to rule over them. There are items amongst the treasure found which have Celtic-style coils and scrolls such as the red enamel hook-escutcheon from a large hanging bowl. The belt buckle, the shield and the reconstruction of the helmet on display at Sutton Hoo all reveal a liking for granulation which was fashionable in Scandinavian work that had possibly been copied from that of the Celts. There is Germanic animal ornamentation which is at the root of much Viking art whose origins flourished in Denmark towards the end of the fifth century, probably in itself influenced by late Roman work. It was from this base that zoomorphic images evolved.

Viking art and its origins is too big a subject for this survey but suffice it to say that there were several styles that developed over the years. A theme that runs through all of them is the intricate nature of it; even a small piece of jewellery could be crammed with myriad figures, most of which appear distorted when compared with real life. The later styles are especially characterised by intertwined and trailing tendrils, delicate foliage, filigree granulation and numerous zoomorphic birds and beasts, many of whom are either biting or disgorging foliage. One of these styles in particular, that known as the Ringerike, was made fashionable in England by the Danish king Cnut (AD 1016–1035). A classic example can be found on a rune-inscribed stone discovered in the churchyard of St Paul's Cathedral, London, and which is now in the Museum of London. It shows a large animal looking back over its shoulder, which is a device also found on the font at Hinton Parva on what is one

33

of the two earliest foliating heads in Christian use that have been found so far in England. The rune stone has tendril-like flowing horns ending in a Celtic half scroll. Its legs have been confused with and are entangled in more trailing foliage whilst its body is bound in delicate interlacing. Its tongue protrudes significantly from its mouth, so much so that it looks as though it has a strand of foliage coming from it.

It can be seen that many cultures in different parts of the world made their mark on the development of art in England. It is usually thought that it most affected church art and architecture rather than that of houses and castles and, although this is likely, it is impossible to prove as a fact because secular art has not survived in such great quantity.

In summary it can only be said that there are no distinct origins of the foliate head. There is no one link that allows an unassailable line-of-descent from a particular artefact, design, story or geographical area. Whether one looks into legend, folklore, other cultures or across continents, sadly nothing can be proved with any confidence, although there are, indeed, numerous possible links. It is notable that the foliate head design is found in such varied forms all over the Catholic West and, as we shall see, in all parts of Christian buildings. It is therefore all the more remarkable that it was routinely ignored by Victorian and Edwardian writers, only apparently coming to prominence in British culture after being renamed Green Men. Many would say that this adds to the allure and mystery of the foliate head, although it is hoped that this brief look at its various potential ancestries shows that, even if Lady Raglan had not coined the term in 1939, the name of Green Man is inappropriate. If the images do come from any of the cultures mentioned above, then the name makes no sense at all.

Wiltshire, Hinton Parva, St Swithun, *c.* 1000.
A foliating animal looks back over its shoulder.

2

Different Types of Foliate Head

Mouth Disgorgers

There are two basic types of foliate head: the disgorgers and the transformers, although it is not as straightforward as that in practice as there are variations on the themes. The disgorgers are certainly the biggest group, making up just under 80 per cent of all the ones found so far whether in this country or overseas. You might therefore expect the transformers to make up 20 per cent but, in fact, 6 per cent of the total both disgorge and transform, as was discussed in the Introduction.

Just over two-thirds of the 80 per cent have the foliage coming out of the mouth, usually from the centre, but it might be from each corner or from just one side of the mouth. When that is the case, it looks as though the carver designed it like that to fit into a corner, as at Guiting Power in Gloucestershire or Adstock in Buckinghamshire, so it is unlikely that anything can be read into it. Usually the mouth is almost shut so that the lips close round the foliage stem or branch but, of this group within a group, a third have their mouths wide open and occasionally teeth can distinctly be seen. As an aside, the average number of teeth per head when they are visible is five, with none of them being jagged or unsightly. As a general rule medieval monsters have excellent teeth, which may not have been the reality of life at that time.

The mouth, of course, is important and we could not survive without it; it is multi-functional being the site of ingestion and expulsion in the sense of feeding and vomiting, of communication in the sense of talking and sometimes for inhalation if the nose is blocked. In some cases, it is hard to decide if the foliage is coming from deep within the stomach as in the case of one on a church in Durham which would chime with *The Golden Legend* story of Adam's death already mentioned. More often one wonders if greenery is being blown out of the mouth, in which case it might have a theological function. Could the leaves coming from the mouth (in this instance) represent the Word of God as in the Gospels or perhaps be a Pentecostal reference? If so, then the whole image would be one of evangelising, of spreading the Word, which might be appropriate for a head on the now-deconsecrated church of St Mary in York since it is on a corbel almost at eye level on the outside of the building and so is very easily accessed by the public. This

Sussex, Little Horsted, St Michael, *c.* 1400.
Disgorging head in an exterior spandrel.

Gloucestershire, Guiting
Power, St Michael and All
Angels, *c.* 1400.
Disgorging from one side of
the mouth.

Buckinghamshire, Adstock, St Cecilia, *c.* 1100.
Disgorging from one side of the mouth.

Staffordshire,
Stafford, St Chad,
c. 1150.
Wonderful teeth!

Cornwall, Lezant,
St Briochus, *c.* 1500.
A clockwise
arrangement
around a head with
good teeth.

County Durham,
Durham,
St Nicholas, *c.* 1400.
An exterior corbel
with deeply
rooted foliage.

Yorkshire, York, St Mary,
c. 1400.
An exuberant head
appears to blow
out foliage.

carving dates to around 1400 which militates against this idea because this was the time of a heresy known as Lollardy. In simple terms, Lollards sought to preach the Gospels in the vernacular which, curiously to twenty-first-century minds, was a heresy. Preaching and exegesis was the sole domain of those who had been trained (i.e. priests); the Word of God was held to be so important that it could not be trusted to the rabble of untutored minds. This particular foliate head is so easily observed that the incumbent could not have failed to have noticed it as soon as he walked round the building, so if it is intended to be blowing out words in an evangelical sense, it seems possible that it would have been removed or amended.

Naturally enough, some of the heads that have their mouths open also reveal the tongue, which is problematic when it comes to analysis. It could be symbolic or just playful, in the same spirit as a child sticking out a tongue. There are several interpretations of what are known as tongue-pulling heads whether or not they belong to a Green Man. An obvious one might be not to slander anyone or tell lies which could tie into biblical texts such as Psalm 11.4, 'May the Lord destroy all deceitful lips, and the tongue that speaketh proud things' or Proverbs 15.4, 'A peaceable tongue is a tree of life: but that which is immoderate, shall crush the spirit'. This is not so much a negative portrayal of the tongue as an observation that man's tongue can run away with him and that unkind words can be uttered without enough thought. The presence of a tongue must surely suggest speech or maybe inhibited speech since you cannot speak whilst sticking out your tongue.

There are a few cases, such as at St Margaret's, Herefordshire, where it is hard to decide if the head has a tongue or if it is tongue-shaped foliage but, generally, where there is a tongue it is clearly identifiable, as on the roof boss in Hadleigh in Suffolk.

Herefordshire,
St Margaret, 1520.

Suffolk, Hadleigh,
St Mary, fifteenth
century.
A disgorging head on a
roof boss which shows a
large tongue as well.

Ear Disgorgers

A few heads (just over 5 per cent) have foliage coming from their ears. There are two distinct styles amongst the ear-disgorgers. The early group, up to about the year 1200, are generally wide-mouthed, goggle-eyed, cat-like beasts, often on fonts. The heads are linked by continuous granulated strands which do not always resemble any specific type of plant. The later group, after 1200, reveal a wider range of styles commensurate with the tastes of the time; some of these heads are much more identifiably human.

Ear-disgorgers seem to generate multiple heads in one place, but at Holt, Iffley, Morville, Kilpeck, Stottesdon and Lewes, which are all 1200 or earlier, the heads are linked to each other by tendrils coming from the neighbouring head's ears. In these cases the heads are not always identical but are often very similar to each other. As a technicality, the heads at Morville are also stylised and do not have precise ears, but the looping tendrils exit the head both at the mouth and at the point where the ears should have been (see the image on p. 32). It is noticeable that multiple heads, linked by circular stylised foliage, very often granulated, were in vogue up to about the year 1200 but as yet there is no explanation for this, other than fashion. It has already been observed that granulation was a popular decoration in Scandinavian, Celtic and classical art so this is most likely to be an influence brought by settling Vikings who also enjoyed depicting heads with tendrils issuing from the mouth.

The ear is, of course, the organ of hearing, so the fact that it has foliage coming from it, thereby blocking it, could indicate a form of deafness. It was also a symbol of betrayal in the

Oxon, Iffley, St Mary, 1175.
Foliage issues from the ears and mouth.

Shropshire, Stottesdon, St Mary, 1160.
Monsters on a font linked to each other by stylised patterns coming from their ears.

Garden of Gethsemane because Peter drew his sword and cut off Malchus' ear at the moment that Judas betrayed Christ. Ears are a means of enslavement as we see in Exodus 21:6, one of several examples where it says, 'His master ... shall bore his ear through with an awl: and he shall be his servant forever', but this does not seem to be relevant to foliate head carvings where a sense of the head being pinned by the foliage leaving the ear has yet to be found. In each case the foliage, stylised or otherwise, enters or exits via the centre of the ear, so there is no suggestion that the foliage is any kind of adornment as an earring might be when attached to a lobe. The intriguing set of four heads round the top of a column at Woodbury in Devon date to around 1300. They are all disgorging human heads, but one issues leaves from both ears and another from the right-hand side of his mouth and from his left ear. This foliage, which comprises stylised vines and grapes, is being eaten by an elegant dragon which emerges vigorously from the left side of a third head's mouth. The dragon has various interpretations depending on context and type, but it was usually held that the danger came from a swipe from its tail rather than any fire from its mouth and so a dragon with a curled or knotted tail has been neutralised. The Woodbury dragon's tail is straight and so it is still viable as a threat. It eats the grapes, the product of the vine and a symbol of the blood of Christ, so this set of heads could be construed as the devil within man attacking the good that is also within him: man's dual nature and the constant struggle between good and evil.

Devon, Woodbury, St Mary, *c.* 1400.
A mouth disgorger on a capital.

Devon, Woodbury, St Mary, *c.* 1400.
Another head disgorges a dragon.

Devon, Woodbury, St Mary, *c.* 1400.
More foliage issues vigorously from a mouth on the same capital.

At Elstow Abbey in Bedfordshire a well-dressed, young, bearded man leans out of a large corbel. He has a mass of somewhat stretched oak leaves coming from his ears and swirling above his head. His eyes are genial, but his expression cannot be accurately assessed because a large but precise rectangle has been removed from where his mouth should be. The damage is smooth and even, suggesting a repair that has never come to fruition rather than defacement. The oak is traditionally a sign of steadfastness in England and the location of this foliate head, one of only thirty-four found in sanctuaries, signifies a position of trust.

The early fourteenth-century head at Dennington in Suffolk is a mouth-pulling, tongue-pulling, distinctly human head. His hands claw at the sides of his mouth whilst his eyes look directly ahead, apparently eagerly. He may be a monk because there is evidence of a fringe on his forehead, but the architecture prevents sight of the top of his head (he inhabits a window capital in the choir) so it is not possible to tell if he is tonsured in the Benedictine fashion or if the hair merely denotes a youngish man. The leaves that issue profusely from his ears appear to be sycamore because two of the propeller-like seeds are also present, the seeds suggesting a renewal of life. Two other foliate heads are present at Dennington, but their plants are hawthorn and peony.

Overall, the ear-disgorging heads are very varied in style, especially after the year 1200. All the later ones are distinctly human, whereas there was a preference for monsters before 1200. (An exception are the seemingly upside-down ones on the de la Warre chantry in

Bedfordshire, Elstow Abbey, St Mary and
St Helena, *c.* 1300.
Foliage comes from the ears of a young man.

Suffolk, Dennington, St Mary, 1330.
A man pulls at his mouth whilst foliage
comes from his ears.

Boxgrove Priory, but they are another red herring since they are part of the de la Warre
family heraldry.) This is not uncommon, although in the case of the ear-disgorgers it seems
to have been to make it easier to carve chains of linked heads. What the overall message
was is not particularly clear: maybe that they were all linked in the same belief, thought
or shared life on earth. Many of them show great imagination, but none of them take us
closer to an overall interpretation.

Nose Disgorgers

Almost 4 per cent of the total number had greenery coming from the nose, sometimes
in conjunction with other orifices. Indeed, the previously mentioned tomb of St Abre at
Saint-Hilaire in Poitiers falls into this category. There is an excellent example on the corbels
of the porch at Castor in Cambridgeshire. The comparatively small British group has
occasionally been cited as providing the original meaning of the foliate head because it is

Cambridgeshire, Castor,
St Kyneburgha, 1120.
A nose disgorger on a
doorway capital.

said to feature in the Bible, in Ezekiel 8.16–18: 'and behold they put a branch to their nose', which may refer to idolaters to whom God would show no mercy. The phrase in context is:

> And he brought me into the inner court of the house of the Lord: and behold at the door of the temple of the Lord, between the porch and the altar, were about five and twenty men having their backs towards the temple of the Lord, and their faces to the east: and they adored towards the rising of the sun. And he said to me: Surely thou hast seen, O son of man: is this a light thing to the house of Juda, that they should commit these abominations which they have committed here: because they have filled the land with iniquity and have turned to provoke me to anger? and **behold they put a branch to their nose**. Therefore, I will also deal with them in my wrath ...

These are ambiguous verses. There is a possibility that they concern Judaic ceremonies connected to a sun-related ritual that has since passed into obscurity. That being so, it seems unlikely to have triggered an image that became current in Christian churches from the early to late Middle Ages across Europe, even though ideas from other spiritual practices were absorbed into Christian art. Idolatry is abhorred in Judaism and Christianity, not least because the Second Commandment tells us that God forbids it. The fear of idolatry, or rather fear of the effects of it, has brought about waves of iconoclasm at various times, more in the Orthodox Church than the Catholic one, but there is a fine line between using images as teaching devices, decoration or for assisting in devotions and actually praying to the person portrayed. If the foliate heads that have branches coming out of their noses are linked to this passage that is possibly about idolatry, then the link seems tenuous for such a serious subject. It would be expected that the message would be expressed in a less subtle way so that the whole congregation would understand it, so it seems that much is being made of a single verse in the Bible.

The data shows a seemingly random placing of foliate heads that involve the nose, and it must be exactly that: there is no overall pattern or logic that has been identified. They range from the very earliest to almost the most recent and are frequently interspersed with more 'normal' ones. The conclusion, again, has to be that there is no special significance that can be attached to a foliate head that has its leaves exiting via the nose. It seems more likely that it was an artistic device enjoyed by the carver than any attempt to illustrate a biblical passage or moral.

Eye Disgorgers

The idea of foliage or anything being disgorged from the eyes is uncomfortable and unpleasant, but nonetheless our less-squeamish medieval ancestors produced carvings in which some 1.5 per cent had exactly that, and that does not include the so-called blood-sucker heads which will be looked at later. Usually, the points of issue are at the corners of the eyes, which may make them slightly more acceptable. The fashion – if it can be styled as such – for plant life appearing at the eyes comes later in the medieval phase of their history, the earliest example being found at Warmington, Northamptonshire, dating to *c.* 1290, and the latest at Woolstone, 1475. No examples have yet been found from the Romanesque period, *c.* 1000–1150.

Branches come out of the actual eyes of the Warmington head, not from the corners of them, which would normally put it in the same bracket as the blood-suckers except that the rest of the face is lifelike with an unperturbed expression, belying the discomforting exit points of the plants. The eight that have been annotated as blood-suckers are distinctly cadaverous. The Woolstone head has a stalk of foliage coming from its closed lips as well as two huge fronds from the edge of the eye sockets.

There are numerous biblical references to eyes, whether it is Jacob being described as the apple of the Lord's eye as an expression of endearment in Deuteronomy 32.10, or in relation to remorse ('Mine eye poureth out tears to God', Job 16.20), or expressing mal-intent and other emotions. The most well-known biblical passages concerning eyes are from Exodus 21.23–24 and Matthew 5.29. The first reference is the Book of the Covenant, which lays down rules for punishment and compensation: 'And if her death ensue thereupon, he shall render life for life. Eye for eye, tooth for tooth …'. The second is where Christ lays down the new law in his Sermon on the Mount: 'If thy right eye scandalise thee, pluck it out, and cast it from thee …'. The latter statement concerns adultery, but the mindset of the Middle Ages could have construed that to be a punishment for a different crime, perhaps a serf looking at a nobleman offensively. Blinding was a part of retributive justice, especially in the early medieval period, and any form of blindness was a genuine and persuasive anxiety, underlining again the very natural desire any person would have to protect their eyes, which makes eyes with branches coming from them even more unsettling.

Given these factors, it is perhaps surprising that more was not made of the combination of branches and eyes. The carvers could have exploited and explored ideas about vengeance, worthiness and emotion, which would have worked well with the medieval taste for the macabre and penchant for portraying monstrous ideas and shapes. The eyes are sometimes described in terms of being windows into our souls; people are criticised for

Northamptonshire,
Warmington, St Mary,
c. 1290.

Berkshire, Woolstone, All
Saints, *c.* 1475.
Foliage comes from the
mouth and from the
corners of the eyes.

not smiling with their eyes as well as their mouths and an instant health assessment can be measured by looking to see how bright or dull a person's eyes might be. It can be difficult to assess mood or meaning if the eyes are shielded. The eyes are a crucial part not only of how people live, but how they are received and judged and yet only 1.5 per cent of the images use them as the point of exit. The obvious conclusion to be drawn from this is that either that the foliate head needed to see, or that eye contact with the spectator mattered.

Whole Body Disgorgers

Although by definition a foliate head is usually a disembodied head, needless to say there are variations in which part, or all, of the body is shown. The most common form of these is part of the shoulders or perhaps hands grasping the stems, as at Melbourne in Derbyshire. Again, there are not so many – only just over 2 per cent of the total number found so far. As with all other types of head, they were not confined to a particular area of the country or to a particular part of the church. Foliate bodies are helpful simply because if more than the

Derbyshire, Melbourne,
St Michael and St Mary,
c. 1150.

head can be seen it might be possible to deduce status and/or to place them within society by looking at what they are wearing. Four examples survive from the Romanesque period at Holt in Worcestershire, Wroxham in Norfolk, Linley in Shropshire and Melbourne, and they show very different approaches to the subject, although they all disgorge from the mouth. This demonstrates again that the carver had a free hand, although this is more surprising because at that time the Romanesque style tended to be more uniform, not only in England but across Europe. The two oldest ones are very different from each other. The head at Holt has a lively, wide-eyed human face with his mouth wide open, which must have been carved in deep relief because his eyes, finger divisions and other details are still clearly marked and he was exposed to the elements for some 800 years, although he was re-cut during a restoration in 1859. His body is visible down to his upper torso and elbows, so the folds of his V-necked robe are visible. He struggles with the stylised foliage, gripping it hard as it forges forward and, to some extent, he has conquered it because it appears to be bending backwards. What is also interesting is that he could be wearing a crown. This image has been inspected several times and it remains unclear whether he is meant to be a king or if the top of the capital has been cut into crenelations. The idea of a crown is favoured, largely because the crenelated pattern does not occur anywhere else on the façade. This foliate head is a capital on a doorway column and is surrounded by zoomorphic figures, a coiled serpent and the chevron zig-zag pattern typical of late Norman architecture, so the subject matters are not connected, which is not unusual for this period.

About 140 miles east of Holt, but made at approximately the same time, is the half figure at Wroxham in Norfolk (see the image on p. 50). This is also part of a doorway scheme, now enclosed within a porch. In this case there are three columns on each side of the door, all of which have a double row of heads on the capitals which range from being identifiably human to monsters, with one being too eroded to be certain. The top layer of heads all involve foliage, but mainly in the sense of them balancing on a nest of leaves as opposed to engaging with it. On the bottom layer, the outer images on both sides are of a bifurcated person with no additional detail. The figure nearest to the door on each side is a half-human. The one on the north side is a person who stands upright with his arms thrown upwards and backwards almost as though tossing the fronds which disgorge from his mouth into the air. The two images are different, but both vigorous.

Norfolk, Wroxham, St Mary, *c.* 1100.
Eroded and hard to make out. A whole person disgorges foliage.

Shropshire, Linley, St Leonard, *c.* 1150.
An adorable alien-like figure surrounded by the foliage he issues on a tympanum.

Worcestershire, Holt,
St Martin, *c.* 1100.
This possibly crowned
head holds onto the foliage
coming from the mouth.

The Wroxham foliate head was carved about half a century before the one at Linley in Shropshire. The styles are different, but the general idea is not dissimilar. This time a whole person is represented, standing with his hands on his hips. An abundance of foliage exudes from his mouth, taking up the remaining space. The rest of the design on this north-facing tympanum is of a restrained nature. It is not known if there was a similar image on the other side of the church because there is too much erosion.

Southwell Minster's chapter house is well known for its exceptionally natural carvings of foliage, created in or around the year 1290. There are several heads in spandrels amongst a profusion of oak, bryony, vines, hawthorn, ivy, ranunculus, potentilla, roses and maple. Not all of them are foliate heads; some are heads that look out through garlands of leaves or through branches, and they are not to scale. Of the eight foliate heads discovered, two of them reveal more than just the head, but not much more. One of them disgorges ranunculus from a wide-open mouth. Two birds of an unknown species stand at the bottom right and left of the image, largely shielding the man's clothing from view. He has a thick neck as though he was a manual worker, and a short fringe of hair, suggesting that he might be a tonsured monk. The other head also includes a neck, and some of his upper garments are visible. Ivy exudes from the right-hand side of his mouth, and he has a tortured expression. Three birds inhabit this carving; again, not identifiable, but one of them appears to be a chick being lifted by its scruff by an adult bird, which might indicate renewal of life, as in a new generation being born. The foliate head at Elstow has already been described under ear-disgorgers, but he is a good example of a well-dressed figure who is a foliate head.

One of the most well-known foliate heads has also already been mentioned. He is in Winchester Cathedral, where they have a total of fourteen, most of which are in the stalls

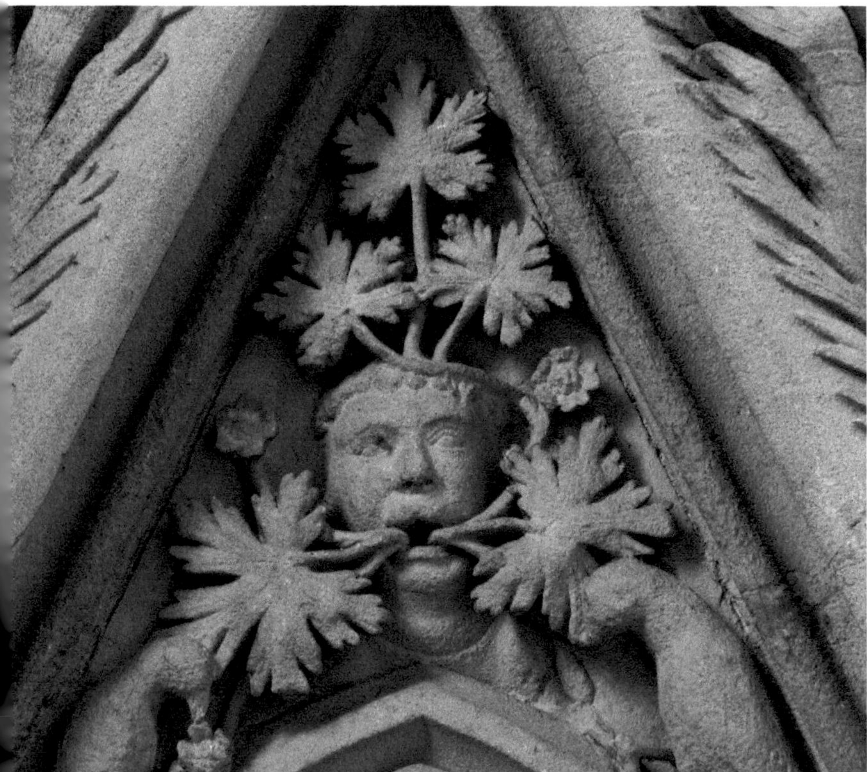

Nottinghamshire, Southwell Minster, St Mary, 1290. Chapter House foliate head with birds. (With kind permission of Southwell Cathedral Chapter)

Nottinghamshire,
Southwell Minster,
St Mary, 1290.
Chapter House foliate head
with birds and a chick.
(With kind permission
of Southwell Cathedral
Chapter)

and carved by William of Lyngwode in 1308. The man is very well dressed, displaying eight small buttons on each cuff, so he is not meant to be a peasant, and he may be wearing boots in a style similar to one of the neighbouring non-foliating fighters. The shape of the spandrel has obliged the carver to put him in a semi-crouching position, as though about to spring up, which is in keeping with his eager glare. Close by, a head with a long neck is wedged into another spandrel, the neck filling the downward point of the triangle. He has his head tipped right back with mouth wide open and some eight good teeth visible, allowing abundant foliage to flow upwards from him into the rest of the space. Both figures have luxurious, thick hair that is worn with a short fringe and a central parting. The hair falls down over their ears into large coils which could not possibly be natural. They appear to be portrayals of the same man, but it is not possible to tell if he is one and the same as the fighting non-foliate head figures because those are wearing what may be balaclava-like headgear.

The Dennington foliate heads are a source of fascination. There are three relevant carvings in this church, two of which are foliate bodies; one of these has been discussed under ear-disgorgers. The other example is definitely of a woman, not only because of the scene depicted, but because she is wearing a wimple – a headdress most likely to have been worn by a religious lady or one of some social status. The flowers issuing from her breasts may be peonies which, in paintings of the Virgin Mary, indicated a rose without a thorn. Whether or not this image qualifies as a foliate head is debatable, although it follows the principle of plant life being dispensed from the body, in this case in a very nurturing way as would be expected if she represents Mary.

Although the majority of foliate heads are human, it is not always possible to assign gender to them. Some of the faces are very smooth, such as that at Podington in Bedfordshire (*c.* 1250). It has arched eyebrows and a small rosebud-lipped mouth. Rope-like tendrils grow from the underside of the nose, ending in stylised leaves curling up and under the ears. It has curly hair, but it is not possible to say if it is long and drawn back or ear length.

Hampshire, Winchester Cathedral, St Swithun, 1308.
A disgorger showing more than just a disembodied head.

Suffolk, Dennington, St Mary, 1330.
A female issuing foliage in a distinctly nurturing way.

Bedfordshire,
Podington,
St Mary, *c.* 1250.
A young-looking
nose disgorger,
possibly female.

Apart from Dennington, the only other likely female head has been found at Lansallos, Cornwall. This is on a bench end of a type that is typical of the West Country and which has Breton influences; it is carved in low relief, the convoluted design taking up the whole of the rectangular panel that forms the end of the pew. In this case, the head is part of a male/female couple, but the male is not foliating. The couple are seen in profile, the woman facing east (the bench end is on the north side of the nave). She has a long nose and appears to be looking down it, but perhaps it is at the single dainty stem that comes out of her mouth, the stylised leaf or bud curling up so that it is almost level with her eyes. The fact that it is heart-shaped might indicate a courtship. She has an exuberant but elegant headdress of single tendrils looped to make bow shapes and she also wears a striking necklace of large beads. Her torso below the necklace is somewhat stylised, as is the man's, but the patterns reflect those of her headdress, if that is what it is meant to be. The man wears a triple-pointed foliate hat of a stylised nature and has his mouth open as though in speech.

The head of around the year 1400 on a transept corbel in Tewkesbury Abbey has been painted gold with some red markings. It is human and looks slightly upwards in a dynamic way. The mouth is open with teeth showing and thick stems exit from each corner. Large, stylised leaves enclose the head, giving an impression of a sketchy tiara. The face is masculine, having heavy features and the short fringe often found on carvings of tonsured monks, but the top part of the torso could be said to be feminine, the light showing plainly that there is some modelling of breasts, although it is equally possible that the carver has merely been clumsy in the way that he has finished the bottom part of the corbel.

Two or three female foliators is a negligible amount, even given the few borderline cases. Nonetheless, they show that the name of 'Green Man' is not appropriate since there are indeed green women. Not one example of a foliating child or baby has been identified so far.

One of the most delightful examples that have more than just the head is at Brant Broughton in Lincolnshire. This is also unique in that no others have yet been found playing a musical instrument. The leaves are neither being disgorged and nor is it necessarily transforming into foliage; instead, it is the hair that has become greenery – a symmetrical mane. The face is serene, the lips slightly parted and concentration appears

Cornwall, Lansallos, St Ildierna, 1490.
A female disgorging foliage on a
bench end.

Gloucestershire, Tewkesbury Abbey,
St Mary, *c.* 1400.
Possibly a female, but not certain.

Lincolnshire, Brant Broughton, St Helen,
c. 1400.
A charming hair transformer playing an
instrument.

to be focused on the instrument, which may be some kind of truncated bagpipe, which he holds at the bottom. Although thin arms and a meagre upper body can be seen, there has been no attempt to indicate dress.

Having examined this particular group of heads in some detail, it becomes clear that there is no traceable thread that connects them. Carvers seem to have been given a free hand in tackling their subject matter and, naturally, some have been more imaginative than others. It is noticeable that there is a lot of energy around the ones that show more than just the head; words like 'vigorous' and 'dynamic' have been used several times. It is also clear that where clothes are visible they seem to be of good quality, with buttons in rows, boots, folds in the cloth and occasionally a fancy neckline. This in turn suggests that the images are high status, an idea borne out by the fact that foliate heads in general are to be found in every cathedral that had the status of cathedral before the Reformation, which applies across Catholic Europe. If they were high status then it follows that they were important, an essential part of the Church's message. The problem lies in discovering what this message might have been.

Foliating Animals

Only 2.5 per cent of the carvings examined were found to have roughly identifiable animals, and these include two twelfth-century beasts on a tympanum at Fritwell in Oxfordshire where chunky monsters disgorge what appear to be whole palm trees. All of the foliating animal heads are disgorgers, presumably so that the carver could show what sort of animal it was. There was both a liking for, and interest in, the symbolism of animals, whether real or imaginary, as seen by the number of bestiaries that survive, the presence of figures from Aesop's Fables on prestigious works such as the Bayeux Tapestry and the quantity of animals shown in medieval art, whether church carvings, murals or manuscripts. There was certainly an affinity between man and beast, which was rightly seen as being crucial for survival.

Eight different types of animals have been found amongst the foliate heads, but it is not clear why these particular ones were chosen. In frequency of appearance, the foliating beasts found are ten dragons, six dogs, four cows, three lions, two weasels, a sheep, a pig and one possible wolf. The most prevalent of the foliating animals is the dragon, of which ten examples were found spread across the centuries and counties. Dragons were universally popular but are also the most difficult to interpret, even given the medieval penchant for opposite meanings depending on the context and for riddles inside riddles.

St Michael slew the seven-headed dragon in the Book of the Apocalypse whilst other dragons attacked by him were defeated and sent down to Hell. St Margaret of Antioch hacked her way out of a dragon's stomach after it had devoured her. Beowulf defeated the dragon in its lair, and there are numerous tales concerning valiant heroes conquering such threatening and ferocious animals. They could be harbingers of misfortune (as in the Viking raids) but also symbols of vainglory and overweening pride. Whilst doing the fieldwork for this survey and visiting numerous churches, it was noticed that of all

Oxfordshire,
Fritwell,
St Olave, *c.* 1150.
Huge beasts
disgorging
tree-like plants.

the many general non-foliating monsters seen, the dragon was omnipresent, so much so that there are even different types of dragons such as wyverns or basilisks. Due to their popularity in medieval art, however, perhaps it should be no surprise that there are more foliating dragons than any other species.

A reptilian dragon climbing inside a spandrel on the west door at Southwold is happily unambiguous. It has spiky wings, claws and scales and is in every way repellent, except for the dainty tendrils coming from its open mouth. The leaves are held carefully between sharp teeth and are certainly foliage, not fire. The position of such a menacing creature would have given a message to those about to enter that they must be on their spiritual guard, and the fact that it is foliating suggests something gentle and different to be found within the building, something to be dealt with care and respect.

An exquisite foliating dragon can be found on the screen at Weston Longville, Norfolk. This Apostles' screen shows the twelve Apostles each holding a scroll with the verse of the Creed attributed to them. There is not room for the whole Creed to be broken down into twelve sections and displayed in full on the screen, so the verses have been abbreviated.

Suffolk, Southwold, St Edmund, 1413.
A foliating dragon.

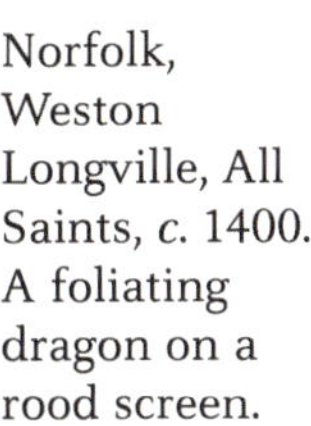

Norfolk, Weston Longville, All Saints, *c.* 1400. A foliating dragon on a rood screen.

Elsewhere, the fillets are filled with peonies and daisies, being symbols of Mary, the dragon being the only exception to that scheme across the whole screen. Richard Lyon had this fifteenth-century screen made, as we know from the inscription '*Ricardi Lyon qui opus fieri fecit*'. The dragon blows foliage at the word *fecit*, which implies that he at least was not averse to such an image so close to what stands as his memorial. In this instance the dragon is in the fillet directly above St Matthew, who holds the words 'He descended into hell; the third day He rose again from the dead', which may be coincidence or may reflect Richard Lyon's hopes that one day he too might rise from death.

All of the dragons have been tamed or contained and remarkably few are fierce, even though one or two sport spikes and savage-looking teeth. The ten examples are spread across three centuries, but the symbolism probably remained the same, which is presumed to be that even the wildest and most unlikely of the people might be saved if they turned to Christianity, that people should be on their guard against spiritual dangers at all times and that no harm could get past the dangerous guardians of the essence of Christianity. Why the foliage was needed is less clear, unless it was to make the point that destructive and aggressive fire had been turned into something recognisably non-threatening which represented life.

Of the six dogs, the most lifelike is that at Over in Cambridgeshire, where some twelve foliate heads adorn the string course that runs round the outside of the church. They are interspersed with tightly closed ball flowers. The dog is seen face on with tendrils coming from each side of its open mouth and looks similar to a modern Labrador with softly drooping ears. In fact, it is assumed to be a talbot, a long-eared hunting dog known for its keen sense of smell, a breed that is now extinct.

Cambridgeshire, Over, St Mary, *c.* 1300.
A realistic dog disgorges stylised plants on an exterior string course.

Devon, Exeter Cathedral, St Peter, *c.* 1300.
A foliating dog at the base of the image, which includes a musical angel and a man falling at the top.

Sussex, Rotherfield, St Denys, 1533.
A horned animal disgorges stylised foliage and dolphins on a font panel.

A rather different disgorging dog is situated at the bottom of an elaborate nave corbel in Exeter Cathedral. The dog is long-eared and probably another talbot. As on all of the Exeter corbels, the foliage rises vigorously and encloses other figures, in this case an angel playing a viol immediately above the dog. Directly above the angel is a man falling downwards, his arms flailing. The most plausible interpretation is that he represents Simon Magus, whose story is told in Acts 8.9–4. He was a magician who was baptised but then fell from grace by attempting to buy what he thought were magical healing powers held by the Apostles. Although he repented, he is usually shown in the act of falling. The dog, in this case, would represent the faithful convert who did not behave in such an unacceptable way.

There are four foliating cows in the survey: a clearly defined one on the string course at Over already discussed; a recently repainted one on a roof boss at the crossing point in Rochester Cathedral; an elegant, gilded one on a nave roof boss in St Mary Redcliffe, Bristol; and a horned one on a panel covering the font at Rotherfield in Sussex where it disgorges stylised fish (probably dolphins) in the Breton manner more often found in the West Country. The Rotherfield one was made at the time of the Reformation in 1533. These have been called cows, but it may be that they were intended to be bulls or even oxen. Cows were important in the Middle Ages, although they never gained the respect and standing found in the Hindu faith, perhaps strangely since they provided meat, milk, leather and vellum. Oxen had higher status, the winged ox being the symbol of St Luke, and they were symbols of strength and achievement. Teams of oxen were common sights in the fields and on the numerous building projects. At Laon, the master mason and people were so impressed by the beasts toiling up the hill with countless cartloads of stone for the cathedral that they honoured them forever by making sixteen, or two teams, of life-size sculptures that look out from the towers over the plains surrounding the city to this day.

Foliating lions may be easier to interpret, which makes it remarkable that so few have been found: three in total at Stoke Dry, Holt in Wiltshire and in Lincoln Cathedral. Unfortunately, the excellent lion at Holt is almost obscured, appropriately, by foliage.

The winged lion is the symbol of St Mark, but in this context other interpretations may be more helpful. Physiologus wrote a collection of tales about animals, not all of them real, in the third century AD and the lion was first on his list. He described it as covering its tracks by swishing its tail to mislead hunters and thus Christ hid himself until he was born to the Virgin Mary. The lion also sleeps with his eyes open so that he is ever vigilant, and it was said that lion cubs were born dead until the father lion breathed life into it on the third day, a clear reference to the Crucifixion and Resurrection. The foliage coming from the lions therefore may represent the new life being breathed into the cub.

The Stoke Dry lion is the most interesting and also one of the oldest in that it was carved *c.* 1100. It is on the northern column of the chancel arch facing into the nave and it teems with carved life. Near the base, a crocodile swallows a hydrus just below the somewhat cartoon-like cat-lion disgorging foliage – its jaws are visible immediately underneath the lion's back paws. There is a man caught in the branches at the top and, below his right hand, a second disgorging face can be seen.

The crocodile lives both on land and in water so M. W. Tisdall explains that it represents not only the dual nature of man, but also the necessity of passing through death to life in his book *God's Beasts*. The hydrus is supposed to roll itself into a ball, slip down the crocodile's

Wiltshire, Holt, St Katherine, *c.* 1400.
A foliating lion obscured by foliage.

Lincolnshire,
Lincoln
Cathedral,
St Mary,
c. 1400.
Vigorous
leaves come
from a lion's
mouth on a
misericord.

Rutland, Stoke Dry, St Andrew, *c.* 1100.
A foliating lion standing on a hydrus at the chancel arch.

Kent, Wye, St Martin and St Gregory, *c.* 1350.
An exterior pig corbel.

throat and then eat its way out, which is taken to be an analogy of Christ descending to Hell and rising again. The whole of the column that is not taken up with livestock or human faces is a mass of intertwined, entangled branches, showing a Scandinavian influence. The story to be read here is about Christ's Passion and ultimate resurrection, the last part being denoted by the foliating lion breathing life into the whole scene.

One foliating pig was found, a somewhat cartoon-like representation on a string course corbel on the outside of the church in Wye in Kent, a place where, coincidentally but appropriately, there was later to be a school of agriculture. The pig is seen face on with thriving, stylised leaves issuing from under its snout. There is another foliate head nearby, but that is a more normal head which disgorges vigorously and wears a small hat. Pigs were (and sometimes still are) associated with gluttony, lust, selfishness, obstinacy and ignorance, so this head could be there to offer moral guidance to the locals; its position on the church's west end renders it visible from what is now the main road, and it was close to the market area then. Swine were both unclean in themselves and in their spirits in the Bible. The dietary laws laid down in Leviticus 11.7 and Deuteronomy 14.8 forbade the eating of pork, but that did not apply to Christians in the West; indeed, pork was a more popular meat than lamb, although that may have been because it was better suited to being preserved to offset winter shortages. Despite this potentially life-saving quality, the pig was despised. They like to wallow in mud, they are unlovely and their hides were too coarse and thick to be made into parchment. The gospels of Matthew, Mark and Luke all tell the story of the Gadarene swine in which evil spirits were summoned from, variously, one or two possessed men and transferred to a herd of about 2,000 swine which then ran down a slope to a lake or into the sea where they drowned.

An ambiguous animal was found on the font at Hinton Parva, which was mentioned earlier in this book. It is thought to date to *c.* 1000, which would mean that it is the second-oldest foliate head in the country found so far (see the image on p. 34) and it is most likely that the animal is a wolf. The wolf fascinates because it looks much like man's best friend but is far more dangerous. They are reckoned to share many of a dog's qualities, being intelligent, fiercely protective and loyal to the pack, but they are also treacherous. The proverb describes someone deceptive as being a wolf in sheep's clothing, which is a biblical reference from Matthew 7.15, which shows the wolf as deceitful because we are warned to beware of false prophets 'which come to you in sheep's clothing, but inwardly they are ravening wolves'. Wolves are shown licking their paws on the lower border of the Bayeux Tapestry and on at least one misericord carving (in Faversham). This is thought to be to soften them to avoid alerting hunters to their presence. It is therefore indicative of their cunning. There are several animal figures present, but the wolf is the only one that is foliating, the vegetation again being in a Scandinavian style. If it is a wolf, its presence on a font may be to show how rapacious greed can be conquered by baptism.

The other figures on this font are easier to define. There are serpents and two cockerels, which either represent a warning not to deny Christ as St Peter did before the cock crowed or signifies vigilance to be awake enough to see the coming of the Messiah. It has not been possible to identify the species of a third bird, although it may be a dove, which would fulfil Christ's promise in Matthew 10.16 when he says, 'Behold I send you forth as sheep in the midst of wolves: be ye therefore wise as serpents, and harmless as doves', which is an appropriate sentiment for a font.

The serpent has several interpretations according to context: it can be temptation because of its role in the Garden of Eden or it can be medicine because of Moses' rod. It is also associated with Christ's resurrection because it sheds its skin, and this is the most likely reason for it being on a font. There are fish present, which are symbols of Christ and feature in many New Testament stories, some of the Apostles being actual fishermen as well as being recruited to be fishers of men. The rebus ICHTHUS is the Greek word for fish, but it can be read as Iesous Christos Theou Huios Soter (Jesus Christ, Son of God, Saviour), which became almost as popular an emblem as the cross, especially in years of persecution.

What is clear is that the images associated with the foliating animal are largely connected to the Passion (the cockerel), the Holy Spirit (the dove) and Christ (the serpent and the fish) and therefore are a long way from ideas about pagan fertility rites.

Devon, Ottery St Mary, St Mary, *c.* 1350.
A blood-sucker head. A cadaver but the foliage is breaking into new life.

Blood-Sucker Foliate Heads

It is not known when and where this term began, although it is descriptive of a type that form a distinct group. In the course of the research for this book around 1,200 foliate heads were examined of which some 725 were made between approximately 1350 and the Reformation of the 1530s, although allowance must be made for heads that have been lost to us from the earlier period. The liking for foliate heads appears to have gone in and out of fashion over the centuries, but it looks as though they were coming back as an art form at the same time that the population was suffering disastrous reverses, whether through famine or a general insufficiency of food. In the face of this misery, comfort of a sort may have been found in foliate head carvings.

There is a particular sub-group known as blood-suckers, which make up only 0.68 per cent of the whole. They are all disgorging heads which have foliage coming from their eyes along with at least one other orifice, usually the mouth but, as in the case of Ottery St Mary, the nose as well. Although disgorging from the eyes has been discussed, the blood-suckers are distinct because the foliage blinds them, giving an impression that it is actually growing

Devon, Axbridge, St John the Baptist, *c.* 1450.
A blood-sucker roof boss.

from within the skull. They are a phenomenon found predominantly in the south-west and west, though two are in Lincolnshire, but no explanation has been found for this other than local fashion. They cannot have been carved by one person and nor are they similar enough to have come from the same workshop. The heads are all human and in varying stages of decay, ranging from the cadaver-like ones at Ottery St Mary and Axbridge to the apparently healthy at Crediton and Spreyton.

An earliest possible date of 1345 has been assigned to Ottery St Mary because the main building of the church was completed in 1342 with the Lady Chapel – the site of the foliate head – being added a few years later. It is likely that it was made *c.* 1350. This head was repainted in the twentieth century and it is not known if any original colour remained to guide the restorer's hand. It is currently cadaver-white and issuing gold stylised leaves from

Devon, Crediton, Holy Cross, *c.* 1400.
A blood-sucker corbel.

Lincolnshire, Stamford, St Mary, 1484.
A gilded blood-sucker head.

all orifices. The leaves are accompanied by equally stylised fruit which is taken to symbolise the culmination of life. At Crediton, a comparatively young face seems almost to be slumbering on a nave corbel whilst a haggard elderly head is part of a stone screen in Marston. Stamford hosts a gilded blood-sucker roof boss in St Mary's whilst the crowned head at Spreyton is found on a roof boss in the chancel which will be looked at separately. Their date is of interest if the Ottery St Mary example was made after 1348 because that means that they all postdate the arrival of the plague commonly known as the Black Death in England, when there was inevitably an increased interest in portraying death, perhaps as a way of coming to terms with it.

These few heads may help with an overall interpretation simply because they are cadavers that exude life. It has been noted before that no matter what the date, style or situation of the head, the foliage is always living and, indeed, it is often vigorous. No example has been found where that is not the case, and they are sometimes accompanied by fruit, new leaves or berries. It may be that the increase in numbers of them in churches indicates that they served as counselling tools in the face of sudden death: whoever looked at them might understand that whatever their short-term fate, in the long term life (eternal life) would come out of them, just as the leaves issue from the heads. This would have been a message understood by largely agricultural communities.

3

Locations

Exterior

It is not uncommon to find one or more Green Men alongside what might be called normal heads, especially amongst roof bosses or in the misericord carvings such as at Cley, Norfolk, where the elegant Green Man is discreet and might not be noticed immediately. Sometimes one or several Green Men are part of a suite of images which can help with their interpretation, but at other times there seems to be no obvious reason why they were placed where they were.

Having once overheard someone say that Green Men could only be on the exterior of a church because priests would never tolerate such an overtly pagan image inside, the author was minded to check. An extensive study was made over several years, at the end of which it was possible to say that only just under 30 per cent of the total examined were on the outside and these were not found to be uniformly placed. Porches and doorways are popular sites, with very few having them on the door itself such as at Higham in Kent. Otherwise, they were found to be on door corbels, beside windows and in voussoirs as part of a tympanum over a door as at Healaugh, Yorkshire. The voussoirs are the wedge-shaped stones that form an arch and they are often decorated seemingly randomly. Green Men can occasionally be found in spandrels beside a door (the triangular-shaped in-filling spaces where there is an archway within a rectangular shape) or, gloriously, as part of an exuberant string course such as at St Mary's at Over, Cambridgeshire, where over a dozen wreath the porch and south side of the church, including the foliating dog. It is evident that some of the images have been moved over the centuries which makes them harder to assess. St Andrew's at Quidenham in Norfolk has a fine example of a disgorger, but it has the air of just having been stuck where a drip stone might once have been to the north of the round tower.

It is not possible to be certain since so many exterior images are now much eroded, but it looks as though this approximate one-third ratio has always generally been the case over the centuries. In the twelfth century the ratio of foliate heads inside and outside was roughly 60:40 whereas later it became about 70:30. That is not a significant difference and probably just shows a shift in fashion.

Norfolk, Cley, St Margaret, *c.* 1350.
A head with foliage coming from the mouth very discreetly.

Kent, Higham, St Mary, fifteenth century.
One of several heads on the actual door.

Yorks,
Healaugh,
St John the
Baptist,
c. 1150.
A strange
configuration
of stylised
leaves on a
voussoir.

Norfolk,
Quidenham,
St Andrew,
c. 1400.
A foliate
head that has
been moved.
Its original
position is not
known.

Interior

To explore the true glories of foliate heads it is better to look at the ones inside the buildings, not least because the chance of their having been eroded is much reduced. That said, it can be all-but impossible to see ones supposedly hidden in the roof, although it is unlikely that they were designed to be less visible. It was found that the most common place for the images inside Christian buildings is in the nave, although that is a rather broad term. The nave, the western part of the church, often doubled up as a village hall where secular events might take place. As roughly 40 per cent of the heads found inside are somewhere in the nave then, whatever message they conveyed, it must have been intended for the congregation as much as the clergy.

One might expect capitals to be the most popular place to find Green Men but that is not the case. In the churches visited, it was found that more than twice as many of them were on roof bosses. Capitals are relatively easy to see today, especially as many are almost at eye level, whereas roof bosses involve much craning of necks and straining of eyes. That might not always have been the case. Whilst the roof boss heads are most commonly in the nave, they are also to be found in the chancel (the choir) and the sanctuary (the most sacred part of the church which houses the high altar). They are often in the transepts – the 'arms' of the church, stretching from north to south) or they might be in individual chapels, inside towers or ambulatories (the one-way system designed for pilgrims to walk behind the high altar in a cathedral). Wherever they might be, it is often said that the heads were hidden deliberately because the medieval craftsmen only worked for the glory of God. This has elements of truth, but it must be said that despite the staunchly Catholics times, medieval craftsmen worked for money so that they could live – as do we all. If they really wanted to hide the Green Men we should expect to find them in roof cavities where these is no decoration or perhaps at the base of a spire cross, but this is not the case. The images were not stowed away, but placed right in the midst of the people.

Many of the carvings still bear traces of colour and, very often, gold leaf or paint. That makes their positioning rather different. Far from being hidden away to become liminal images, foliate heads were part of the liturgy. It is hard to get an impression today when so much colour has come off the carvings, leaving them a bare wooden brown set in wooden roofs. If one imagines them glinting with gold leaf or paint, shimmering and flickering in the dancing light of many candles, then one gets an idea of how they might have been as we can see at Tewkesbury Abbey, Brant Broughton, Stamford and numerous other places.

Fonts

Fonts and tombs both host foliate heads, there not only for the start and end of your earthly life but also the beginning of your Christian life and access to eternal life beyond. The Church observes Seven Sacraments, but baptism is one of the two ordained by God (Matthew 28.19). To die unbaptised was a terrible thing in the Middle Ages, so pictorial messages carved on fonts might be protective, positive but also terrifying, as at Luppitt in Devon which has a spectacular Scandinavian-style monster disgorging stylised foliage.

Devon, Luppitt, St Mary, *c.* 1075.
A dramatic foliating monster on a font.

Anyone approaching this font (and acceptance into Christianity) would be aware that good behaviour was required, although there is something amiable about this monster once one gets over one's surprise.

If the notes in the church in Dolton, Devon, are correct, the head on their font is the oldest found so far in this country, possibly having been made as early as AD 800 and by AD 1000 at the latest. The head is a semi-human, goggle-eyed design which disgorges foliage from its nose in a manner not dissimilar to the oldest one known in a Christian context at Poitiers. It is difficult to see because it is upside-down, not having been designed to be a font originally. It is thought to have been made from blocks from two different Saxon crosses, possibly using stone from Italy. The stonework was restored in 1997 when the upper one was inverted to make a larger and more secure area for the base. Perhaps, therefore, this should not be counted amongst the fonts but as a preaching cross in its own right, which makes the head even more intriguing especially as the surrounding images are interlinked circles and tendrils as opposed to specific pictures. Preaching crosses were widespread in Anglo-Saxon England and a number of examples survive. They were deeply incised, usually with biblical stories as well as some symbolism. Some were used to mark sacred spots, places of prayer and boundaries, whilst a few acted as memorials, and it is thought that the custom began in the early eighth century. It implies that the Dolton head was used to impart a Christian message, even if its precise nature may not now be obvious. It was not uncommon for a

Devon, Dolton, St Edmund, 800–1000.
The foliate head is upside down on this font, which was probably originally part of a preaching cross.

preaching cross to have intricate foliage – often vines – decorating the sides, but this is the only instance found so far of one where foliage engages with a head.

Lullington in Somerset offers a mid-twelfth-century specimen in good condition. It hosts six charming beast heads resting above a wide band encircling the font a third of the way from the top and which is deeply inscribed: '*Hoc fontis sacro pereunt delicta lavabo*' ('In this holy font sins are washed away'). This is the not only inscription associated with a foliate head, but it is specific to the function of the vessel. The heads are not uniform in that some have distinct teeth whilst others look more cat-like, but they all disgorge similar chunky stems in a Scandinavian style. A band of rosettes appears below the inscription, with the rest of the font being taken up by interlinked blind arcade-work of a type reminiscent of canon table pages in manuscripts. It is noticeable that the earlier fonts with foliate heads on them sported more stylised ones, often with the heads linked together and set amongst abstract images. Later on, single heads appear, for example at Bulmer in Essex where a serene face dating to around AD 1400 looks out from stylised vines with oversized grapes that issue from his mouth and corners of his eyes.

Although there are some notable early fonts (Deerhurst, for example), either fonts were not widely installed prior to AD 1100 or they have not survived, which is why there are so few instances of heads on fonts before that date and perhaps accounts for their similarity in style. It seems likely that a portable bowl or indeed a shell was used previously.

Somerset, Lullington, All Saints, *c.* 1150.
Charming, stylised beasts adorn this font, which also has an inscription.

Essex, Bulmer, St Andrew, *c.* 1400.
A font with a large head from which stylised leaves and fruit are issued.

Tombs

More foliate heads have been found on tombs than on fonts, which must surely confound the idea that they should be interpreted as pagan fertility rites. Just as on fonts, sometimes there are multiple examples on tombs and sometimes single ones, presumably according to the wish of the occupant and/or whoever wished to commemorate him. At Rochester, Bishop Hamo de Hethe's tomb sports six. He was bishop of Rochester from 1319 to 1352 until he retired in his eighties because of ill health. His seemingly empty tomb is in the ambulatory of Rochester Cathedral, but his effigy would have lain under a single arch with a quatrefoil apex. The lower border of the arch is decorated with four spandrels containing six foliate heads – five disgorging and one transforming. They are delicately carved and are a mixture of grotesques and humans and one engages with oak leaves. The overall scheme sweeps the heads in an upwards direction, as though travelling heavenwards.

Another priest with a Green Man on his tomb is at Harpswell in Leicestershire. Nothing is known about the rector, William Harrington, other than that he died in 1350, but he has an oversized and somewhat clunky head at the base of his effigy.

The number might be a little disingenuous, though, because thirty-seven font heads have been found on eighteen fonts but forty-one were found on only fourteen tombs. Fourteen tombs bearing Green Men is not an impressive number, but it is enough to show that the

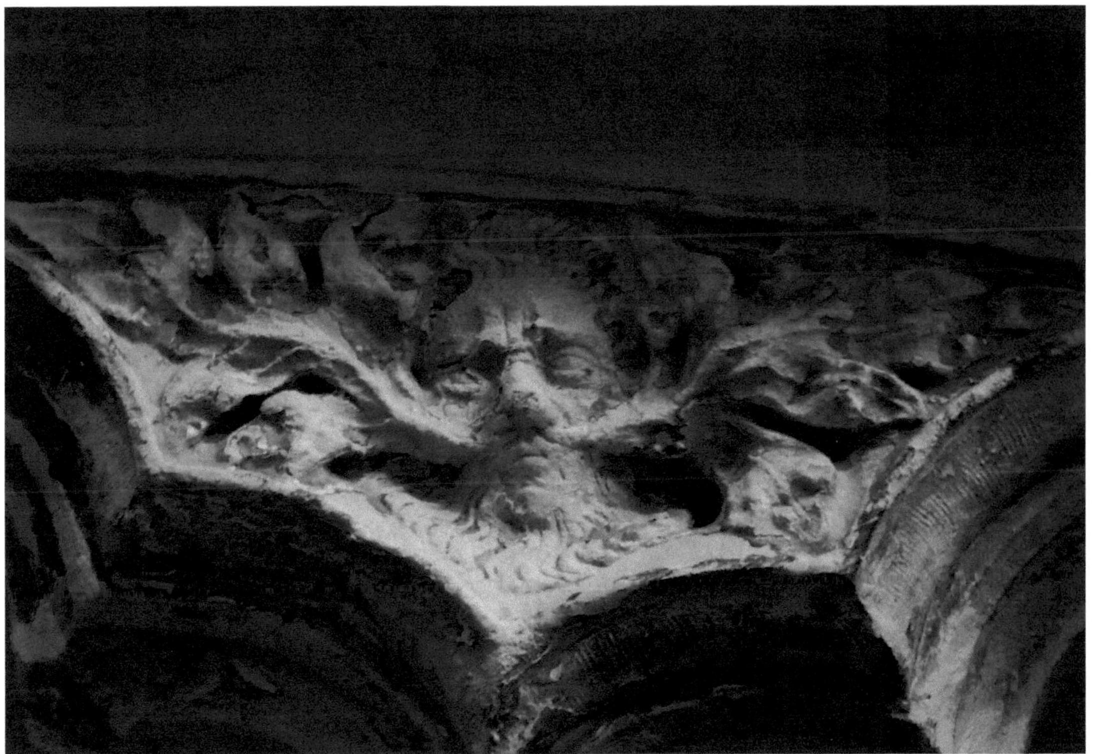

Kent, Rochester Cathedral, Christ and Blessed Virgin, 1352.
Bishop Hamo's tomb. The Chapter of Rochester Cathedral.

Leicestershire, Harpswell, St Chad, 1350.
An effigy of a priest with a large foliate head at his feet.

image was not thought to damage the occupant's chances of reaching the next world. It should also be noted that tombs were occasionally designed by the future inhabitant, which refutes any notion that they were held to be displeasing to God in any way, and some tombs housed holy men. Apart from the case of Bishop Hamo, seventeen stylised, linked heads were found on a grave slab made for Gundrada, who was the wife of William de Warenne and died in 1085. This was not her original tomb because she died in childbirth in Norfolk. It seems that she was taken to Lewes in Sussex at some point and a new grave slab made, possibly as part of the building of the new priory church of St Pancras. A lengthy Latin inscription runs around the edges and down the centre, some of which has been lost but which refers to her nobility and purity.

The Middle Ages were a time when planning a funeral was more important than a wedding. There was a sense that an individual's main purpose in life was to ensure that he got not only himself into paradise but his family too, so there was a strong element of responsibility in his piety. It is telling that traditional pre-Reformation religious practices died hard as was found frequently on Episcopal visitations when it was discovered that the people cleaved to the use of candles and the ringing of bells before the funeral to elicit prayers for the dead. There was an aspirational element to one's funeral since burial within the parish church was both socially prestigious and expensive, costing as much as £1 or £2 to carry out the work involved. The number of chantry chapels built and other costly donations to churches evident to this day were all made not so much to be remembered by future generations, but in the hope that it would help their transition to Heaven and to ask those still living to pray for them.

Apart from the great and good of the land, heads of families that were notable locally also planned their tombs – some very beautifully, others less so. The 1450 head in the Goddard Chapel, Aldbourne, is arguably the most repellent of them all, having pocked, reptilian features on a human face. A floor brass commemorates Richard Goddard as a benefactor. This is a sizable and impressive tomb in the south transept of the church, so it is hard to understand why the family went for something so difficult to look at.

Wiltshire, Aldbourne, St Michael, *c.* 1450.
The Goddard family tomb.

Sussex, St George, Crowhurst, 1451.
John Gainsford's tomb.

John Gainsford was also a benefactor, but at Crowhurst, Sussex, dying in 1451. A memorial brass reveals him as a knight, his feet resting on a dog with a Latin inscription stating that he, his wife Anna and son Richard are buried there. Two heads of an unusual type are on this tomb: one is a hybrid, a head with large, pointed ears and stylised foliage emerging from the mouth; the other is a human whose mouth is stuffed with stylised grapes, which also are disgorged on straight stems. Other tombs with foliate heads on them have been less easy to analyse, but the overall message appears to be one of optimism in the sense of a connection to eternal life. St Abre's tomb in Poitiers has already been discussed with the use of acanthus. At the head of her tomb there are more acanthi being dispensed by two highly unconventional dolphins, creatures that were held to be psychopomp – they were there to guide your soul to the next world. This is a mixture of classical, pagan and Christian ideas, but clearly indicating a belief in personal resurrection.

Easter Sepulchres

Easter Sepulchres are comparatively rare; many will have been held to be altogether too Catholic at different times of Christian practice, wooden ones will have crumbled away, whilst others will have been installed annually for the occasion and then removed. In

Christian iconography they are the ultimate tomb since they were designed to be the empty resting place of Christ until his body was symbolically placed there at Easter. To have such sepulchres bearing foliate heads can only be of great interest because of this function and there is an excellent example at Little Leighs in Essex, dating to around 1300.

Easter Sepulchres take the form of ornately decorated canopied recesses, routinely in the north wall of the sanctuary in the chancel. They were used to safeguard the consecrated Host, held to be the actual body of Christ, from Maundy Thursday until the First Mass of Easter, which of course makes them extremely high-status items. That they were in regular use is evident from church wardens' accounts, such as at St Mary Redcliffe, Bristol, in the 1470s where a new one was ordered which had plenty of gold leaf along with images of the risen Christ, the sleeping soldiers, a model of Hell, four angels with wooden wings and God the Father and the Holy Ghost coming from Heaven down to the sepulchre. Good Friday being a day of great mourning, the people would often approach the revealed cross

Essex, Little Leighs, St John the Evangelist, *c.* 1300.
An Easter Sepulchre.

Essex, Little Leighs, St John the Evangelist, *c.* 1300.
Detail of the Easter Sepulchre.

barefoot and on their knees to venerate it, a practice known as 'creeping to the cross' which was scorned post-Reformation. During the First Mass the clergy processed to the Easter Sepulchre from whence the Host was taken and placed on the high altar. The point is that the body of Christ was not only placed in the Sepulchre but housed there and guarded.

At Little Leighs there is a *c.* 1300 effigy of a priest in the place where the body of Christ should be! It is interesting in itself, being the only known wooden effigy of a priest in this country, and although it is stored in what may appear to be a convenient place, it is one that would be of some embarrassment to the occupant. There are two foliate heads on this tomb in opposing spandrels. One is a tongue-pulling, leonine hybrid which disgorges peonies, already shown to be a symbol of Mary. Trails of oversized oak leaves with acorns are draped along the top of the ogee-shaped canopy with a discreet dragon-like monster at each end. In the centre-right spandrel (the one the occupant would see if he opened his eyes) is a head of a bearded man with vigorous wavy hair. He disgorges hawthorn, some of the leaves still curled in bud form, suggesting a new growth. The man looks to be about thirty-three, the age it is believed Christ was when he was crucified. It is possible – indeed likely – that the carver intended to portray Christ as a foliate head, which makes any interpretation of the image extremely positive; pre-Reformation religious practice would not have tolerated any ambiguity about Christ's sacrifice and resurrection. If one examines this sepulchre with the aid of a torch and a magnifying glass, it is possible to detect traces of what is presumed to be the original colour, which is predominantly red, not green.

4

Additional Details

One might expect the types of leaves to be key to interpreting the heads, but that might not be so. Although twenty-seven different species were found, some of which can be analysed (oak represents strength, the vine is the Eucharist and so on), it is a simple fact that all the plants' leaves are lobed, so they are artistic. The only exception found so far is at Beverley, St Mary's, where a man in a simple hat disgorges bay leaves. A list of the plants is below, but not too much emphasis should be placed upon them. It is not as though they are all healing or benign plants since ivy can be poisonous, nor have the carvers shown them to scale. The exquisitely carved foliage at Southwell Minster reveals leaves that are out of proportion to the rest of the plant. Where the species could be identified, it was found that the five most popular plants were (in descending order) oak, hawthorn, vine, maple and acanthus, but it is a prosaic fact that the type of foliage might not mean anything at all since almost 80 per cent of the Green Men found had either unidentifiable or highly stylised greenery. Not one instance was found where the foliage was not thriving and that seems like to be the important factor. Indeed some, such as at Sutton Benger, not only have leaves, but birds and buds as well.

> Plant species found: acanthus, bay, bramble, bryony, buttercup, cabbage, cinquefoil, cranesbill, daisy, dog-rose, elder, elm, hawthorn, hornbeam, ivy, laurel, maple, mugwort, oak, palm tree, peony, potentilla, rose-bay, rose, rowan, sycamore, vine.

That said, occasionally quirky things were found being disgorged. The mermen at Crowcombe have been mentioned, but amongst other things, strange-looking serpents come out of an understandably shocked-looking face at Kilpeck whilst another one wraps itself round a head at Tickencote, Rutland. It is even possible that dogs' and monsters' heads are being disgorged at Cheddar and Weston-in-Gordano in Somerset ... but they also all thrive.

Other additions were headdress of many kinds: caps, cowls, coronets, crowns, hats, headbands, mitres and even a wimple, as we have seen at Dennington. The early crowns include Holt in Worcestershire, which has been discussed elsewhere. There is one at Riccall, Yorkshire, which dates to 1160 and is a capital on a doorway now

Wiltshire, Sutton Benger, All Saints, *c.* 1350.
Foliate head with birds in the foliage.

Herefordshire,
Kilpeck,
St Mary and
St David,
c. 1150.
A strange
beast with
serpents
coming from
its mouth.

Rutland, Tickencote,
St Peter, *c.* 1130.
Stylised leaves and
a serpent engage
with this head on the
chancel arch.

Somerset, Cheddar, St Andrew, *c.* 1500.
Possible dog heads come from the mouth.

enclosed by a porch. The face is eroded, but stylised foliage of a Scandinavian type comes from the ears. The crown is not only in good condition but comprises three crosses set on a band representing the Trinity. It is in company with non-foliating heads which are also much worn. St Nicholas-at-Wade, Kent (*c.* 1175), offers the earliest realistic human faces on an aisle capital. There are two foliate heads that face each other, both having bulbous, almond-shaped eyes, smooth faces and both disgorge stylised foliage, the stems of which are granulated. One of them wears a coronet decorated with three triple-lobed leaves. A few foliate heads with crowns come from the early fourteenth century, pleasing examples being Desborough in Northamptonshire and Hereford, All Saints.

Kent, St Nicholas-at-Wade, St Nicholas, 1175.
A crowned foliate head.

Northamptonshire, Desborough, St Giles, *c.* 1300.
Another crowned foliate head.

Crowned foliating heads can be found on misericords as well. Cartmel Priory's head has a complex crown and is a triple Janus image, of which only the two outer heads disgorge. The original Janus had two faces, looking backwards and forwards, and gave his name to January. A Roman god, he symbolised transition, especially of time; he ruled the birth of gods and also represented vigilance. His use as a foliate head is intriguing especially as he has been crowned, perhaps as king of change. Whilst the stylised foliage appears to be of two different types, it may be intended to indicate the same plant species but at different times of the year.

There are numerous biblical references to crowns. The foliate heads do not appear to be wearing crowns of thorns but diadems, which can be interpreted as symbols of kingship, pride, victory, justice and endurance; indeed, St Benedict remarks in his Rule that endurance brings forth a crown. He may have taken his theme from James 1.12: 'Blessed is the man that endureth temptation; for when he hath been proved, he shall receive the crown of life, which God hath promised to them that love him.' In the Book of Proverbs 17.6 it is noted that children's children are the crown of old men, which implies a different kind of endurance, that of continued existence through future generations. This theme is repeated later in Proverbs 27.24: 'For thou shalt not always have power; but a crown shall be given to generation and generation.' In this context the foliage disgorged by a crowned foliate head could represent new life and creation. St Paul, writing to Timothy (2 Timothy 4.8), refers to a crown of justice which is laid up for those that love the Lord. Both of these references align with the idea of just desserts at last being attained and therefore of endurance being rewarded.

It may be that significance can be attached to foliating crowned heads, which variously could refer to status or to the spiritually positive outcome of endurance, but it is unlikely that anything can be gained from any analysis of hats and caps in general. It seems that the majority were created at the whim of the carver and that they became more sophisticated in style as time passed. The prosaic analysis of the be-hatted foliate heads is, again, that there is no specific significance to be attached to them or, if there was, it has been lost over the centuries.

Conclusion

So much of the analysis of Green Men or foliate heads ends not with a bang but a whimper: clues take us so far along a road but then peter out. One of the pleasures of foliate head-hunting are the endless side roads and paths down which one is led. Although they are in positions of some prestige and in high-status buildings, they are also a minority image, possibly only constituting two or three in every hundred carvings. They have been found in two leading churches in the capital: Westminster Abbey and Temple Church, having been made at times when there was interest in creating new religious buildings and so they would have been influential designs. Heads have been found in every cathedral that had that status before the Reformation, and in some monastic buildings as well as in small parishes, but there does not appear to be any association with town business; no link could be established to markets, for example. It cannot be said that foliate heads were purely for the benefit of the people because of the number that are in chancels and sanctuaries and, likewise, they are not there solely for the clergy. Only a third are on the exterior of the buildings for the benefit of passers-by where they are seemingly randomly placed amongst other carvings of monsters, foliage, saints, biblical stories, Last Judgements and occasional social comment. This apparent scattering holds true for those heads that are on roof bosses and misericords. The location of some in specific sites such as fonts and tombs indicate a positive interpretation for the reasons given, especially those on an Easter Sepulchre.

It was often helpful to try to work out the message the carvers of the foliate heads were trying to send by looking at the context provided by surrounding images (as has been done with the font at Hinton Parva, the column at Stoke Dry, et cetera). Whoever installed the bosses in the chancel at Spreyton in Devon came as close as any of them to making direct links. Here there is a barrel roof with nine bosses in good condition, one being a crowned blood-sucker in the centre of the three on the north side. This links to other bosses showing the Alpha and Omega, the beginning and the end, which speaks for itself. The central boss at the east end, right above the altar, is the Chi Rho: the sacred monogram that is only found in medieval manuscripts in the Gospel according to St Matthew, chapter 1.18, which is where he begins to tell the story of the birth of Christ. In the centre, acting as a link between them all, is a boss that sports the three hares. Also known as the Tinners Rabbits in the West Country, this is a circular motif probably

Devon, Spreyton, St Michael, 1471.
A chancel roof boss with a crowned blood-sucker.

originating from the Middle East or Asia. No one is entirely sure of its meaning, although in a Christian context it is likely to refer to the Trinity. All of these clues point to thoughts about eternal life, as has happened in numerous other suites of images. At Spreyton, it is helped by a long text on the chancel beams, much eroded and abbreviated. Enough remains to be able to pick out such words as '*ora*' and '*laud*' – prayer and praise.

There is a distinct possibility that the interpretation and/or use of the foliate head image changed over the centuries since everything that has been said about the Green Men of the later Middle Ages should be set against a backdrop of climate change and disease. There had been a gradual deterioration in climate that had caused widespread famine in 1315–17, which may have killed as many as 15 per cent of the known world's population whilst having a serious impact on the survivors. Further harvest failure in 1321 brought about more famine, with consequences for prices and mortality. It has been said that the early fourteenth-century population was not just malnourished but 'calamity sensitive' so that by the time the plague known as Black Death reached England in 1348 people were both physically and mentally less able to withstand disease.

Whilst the Middle Ages were disease-ridden years, the impact of this particular sickness can be judged from the many texts that are extant, inscriptions on walls in churches such as Ashwell in Hertfordshire and Acle in Norfolk, a fashion for cadaver tombs, a liking for Three Living Three Dead stories in wall paintings and in a rekindling of interest in images such as the foliate head. Texts survive in the form of chronicles and letters from across Europe, not just from England, many of them describing both the actual disease and its ferocity. It is generally held to have killed half the population in twelve to eighteen months, but the death rate could have reached as high as two-thirds in some places. The disease spread relentlessly, perhaps at the speed a horse and its rider could amble. It must have been like an artillery barrage creeping ever nearer and the terror it inspired can only be imagined. It is plain from surviving texts that individuals believed that plague was God's vengeance on them for their sins. The disease was cyclical, with further outbreaks being recorded in 1361, 1369, 1375 and 1390. Obituary lists show that plague continued into the fifteenth century, occurring in every decade except for the 1490s, but recurring in 1501, 1504 and 1507. The effect of this shocking disease on public and individual psyche must have been profound, but it is against this background that there appears to have been a renewed interest in, and proliferation of, foliate head carving and the introduction of those known as blood-suckers. Far from being leftover pagan fertility rites, it is very possible that clergymen used the heads as a medieval counselling tool in the sense that in a week or even a few days' time, they could all be dead, but not to feel utter despair since out of everyone came life – the foliage that is always thriving and suggesting a new beginning, no bad how an individual might have been in life.

The conclusion is that foliate heads are symbols of eternal life, particularly demonstrated by the thriving leaves. Perhaps the carver at Weston Longville was trying to state that clearly when he placed a delicate foliating dragon on the Apostle screen directly above the image of St Matthew who bears the verse from the Creed that reads 'ascendit in caelum' – ascended into Heaven. Just as Lady Raglan was in Llangwym, so was I in Spreyton, Weston Longville and numerous other churches looking at these strange carvings and trying to reach back into the mindset of the Middle Ages. In the end, the exact explanation of the foliate head remains unfathomable with so many possible origins, so many interpretations according to location in or on a church. That said, where symbolism can be understood it is plain that there are positive connections to resurrection and the next life. It is apparent that there was a swift burst of foliate head carvings coinciding with national and personal hardship when Black Death more than decimated the known world, which in turn must reflect the mood of the time and a cleaving to hope for personal resurrection. It may also, of course, have no meaning – one should never underestimate the playfulness of medieval art.

Acknowledgements

This book has been a long time in the making, not least in taking thousands of photographs from which I have chosen only a few as illustrations. My first thanks must go to those church wardens and custodians who generously turned out to make sure that churches were open and who even more kindly either hung about so that they could lock up or trustingly handed me the sometimes vast keys. Otherwise, my sincere thanks go to those listed below who have seemed interested (even when they could not possibly have been) and given endless encouragement: John Carter, Jackie Cooke, Diana and Steve Delia, Ann Green, Dr Luella Hibbous, Pat May, Dr Sheila Sweetinburgh, Sr Ruth White CSC, my many friends at St Andrew's, Deal, and all of those who have sat through my lectures or been on tour and helped nudge me into what I hope is a better perspective on the subject. My husband, Gordon, has been heroic, patiently listening to the ups and downs of it all, not to mention driving endlessly; he must have sat outside more churches than any other man alive. Gigantic thanks to and in memory of David Spenceley.